1st EDITION

Perspectives on Modern World History

The Great Society

1st EDITION

Perspectives on Modern World History

The Great Society

Scott Reid

Editor

GREENHAVEN PRESS
A part of Gale, Cengage Learning

GALE
CENGAGE Learning·

Farmington Hills, Mich • San Francisco • New York • Waterville, Maine
Meriden, Conn • Mason, Ohio • Chicago

Patricia Coryell, *Vice President & Publisher, New Products & GVRL*
Douglas Dentino, *Manager, New Products*
Judy Galens, *Acquisitions Editor*

For more information, contact:
Greenhaven Press
27500 Drake Rd.
Farmington Hills, MI 48331-3535
Or you can visit our Internet site at gale.cengage.com.

For product information and technology assistance, contact us at
Gale Customer Support, 1-800-877-4253.

For permission to use material from this text or product, submit all requests online at
www.cengage.com/permissions.

Further permissions questions can be e-mailed to permissionrequest@cengage.com.

Articles in Greenhaven Press anthologies are often edited for length to meet page requirements. In addition, original titles of these works are changed to clearly present the main thesis and to explicitly indicate the author's opinion. Every effort is made to ensure that Greenhaven Press accurately reflects the original intent of the authors. Every effort has been made to trace the owners of copyrighted material.

Cover images © Everett Collection Inc./Alamy and © Washington Bureau/Hulton Archive/ Getty Images.

LIBRARY OF CONGRESS CATALOGING-IN-PUBLICATION DATA

The Great Society / Scott Reid, book editor.
   pages cm
  Includes bibliographical references and index.
  ISBN 978-0-7377-7308-8 (hardcover)
 1. United States--Politics and government--1963-1969. 2. United States--Politics and government--1963-1969--Sources. 3. Johnson, Lyndon B. (Lyndon Baines), 1908-1973. 4. United States--Economic policy--1961-1971. 5. Economic assistance, Domestic--United States--History--20th century.
6. United States--Social policy. 7. Social legislation--United States--History--20th century. I. Reid, Scott, 1986-
  E846.G735 2015
  320.097309'04--dc23

2014033425

Printed in the United States of America
1 2 3 4 5 6 7 19 18 17 16 15

CONTENTS

CHAPTER 2 Controversies Surrounding Great Society
Programs

Deal-type programs and Great Society entitlements. He writes that the latter increase budget deficits and encourage the degradation of the family structure.

A former health-care official argues that to save Great Society programs, reforms are needed that address Americans' longer life expectancy.

An expert on nonprofit organizations explains the enduring contributions made by key components of the War on Poverty and their effect on American society and institutions. He also argues for advocacy as an integral part of social services.

An education expert reviews the changes in US colleges and universities since the mid-1960s. He reports that enrollment of women and minorities has increased, but completion rates differ significantly by race and gender.

A historian reviews the development of the National Endowment for the Arts and the National Endowment for the Humanities and argues that there is an important role for the federal government in the funding of culture.

An early childhood development professor reviews the ideological underpinnings of Head Start and its relationship to the War on Poverty and the civil rights movement. In her analysis, the greatly beneficial program has developed the standards for understanding child development and learning.

The president of the United States commemorates the anniversary of the Civil Rights Act of 1964 by stating his belief that government can foster social progress and exhorting Americans to continue to work on the promise of the Great Society.

A teacher shares her story of serving in the Volunteers in Service to America program. On assignment in Arkansas, she encountered prejudice and animosity, but was able to help others and learn valuable lessons.

FOREWORD

"History cannot give us a program for the future, but it can give us a fuller understanding of ourselves, and of our common humanity, so that we can better face the future."

—Robert Penn Warren,
American poet and novelist

The history of each nation is punctuated by momentous events that represent turning points for that nation, with an impact felt far beyond its borders. These events—displaying the full range of human capabilities, from violence, greed, and ignorance to heroism, courage, and strength—are nearly always complicated and multifaceted. Any student of history faces the challenge of grasping the many strands that constitute such world-changing events as wars, social movements, and environmental disasters. But understanding these significant historic events can be enhanced by exposure to a variety of perspectives, whether of people involved intimately or of ones observing from a distance of miles or years. Understanding can also be increased by learning about the controversies surrounding such events and exploring hot-button issues from multiple angles. Finally, true understanding of important historic events involves knowledge of the events' human impact—of the ways such events affected people in their everyday lives—all over the world.

Perspectives on Modern World History examines global historic events from the twentieth century onward by presenting analysis and observation from numerous vantage points. Each volume offers high school, early college level, and general interest readers a thematically arranged anthology of previously published materials that address a major historical event, with an emphasis on international coverage. Each volume opens with background information on the event, then presents the controversies surrounding that event, and concludes with first-person narratives from people who lived through the event or were affected by it. By providing primary sources from the time of the event, as well as relevant commentary surrounding the event, this series can be used to inform debate, help develop critical thinking skills, increase global awareness, and enhance an understanding of international perspectives on history.

Material in each volume is selected from a diverse range of sources, including journals, magazines, newspapers, nonfiction books, personal narratives, speeches, congressional testimony, government documents, pamphlets, organization newsletters, and position papers. Articles taken from these sources are carefully edited and introduced to provide context and background. Each volume of Perspectives on Modern World History includes an array of views on events of global significance. Much of the material comes from international sources and from US sources that provide extensive international coverage.

Each volume in the Perspectives on Modern World History series also includes:

- A full-color **world map**, offering context and geographic perspective.
- An annotated **table of contents** that provides a brief summary of each essay in the volume.
- An **introduction** specific to the volume topic.
- For each viewpoint, a brief **introduction** that has notes about the author and source of the viewpoint, and that provides a summary of its main points.
- Full-color **charts, graphs, maps**, and other visual representations.

- Informational **sidebars** that explore the lives of key individuals, give background on historical events, or explain scientific or technical concepts.
- A **glossary** that defines key terms, as needed.
- A **chronology** of important dates preceding, during, and immediately following the event.
- A **bibliography** of additional books, periodicals, and websites for further research.
- A comprehensive **subject index** that offers access to people, places, and events cited in the text.

Perspectives on Modern World History is designed for a broad spectrum of readers who want to learn more about not only history but also current events, political science, government, international relations, and sociology—students doing research for class assignments or debates, teachers and faculty seeking to supplement course materials, and others wanting to improve their understanding of history. Each volume of Perspectives on Modern World History is designed to illuminate a complicated event, to spark debate, and to show the human perspective behind the world's most significant happenings of recent decades.

INTRODUCTION

US president Lyndon B. Johnson made poverty and injustice the focal point of his domestic policy and hoped to improve the economic and societal conditions of American minorities, immigrants, and the poor. Following his inauguration, an incredible amount of legislation was quickly passed that took on the name of the Great Society, from a speech Johnson gave at Ohio University on May 7, 1964: "With your courage and with your compassion and your desire, we will build a Great Society. It is a Society where no child will go unfed, and no youngster will go unschooled."

During his first State of the Union address on January 8, 1964, Johnson outlined a plan to reduce poverty in the United States that was given the unofficial name of the War on Poverty. Following the speech, Congress passed the Economic Opportunity Act, which allowed a federal agency named the Office of Economic Opportunity to divert federal funds to local programs that would reduce poverty in America's poorest communities. Some of these programs, such as Job Corps and Head Start, were antecedents to programs that still exist today.

The Great Society had a stunning effect on modern American life. Included in the banner legislation of the program are the Civil Rights Act of 1964, the Voting Rights Act of 1965, the Elementary and Secondary Education Act of 1965, the Higher Education Act of 1965, the Social Security Act of 1965, and the Public Broadcasting Act of 1967. Dozens more pieces of legislation were passed during Johnson's administration that continue to affect American life five decades later.

The Great Society has been a divisive facet of American society since its inception in 1964. Conservative commentators continue to cite it as the catalyst that caused several government programs to snowball into a massive bureaucracy that funnels an extraordinary amount of money into programs that do not help the less-fortunate. They argue that this creates a welfare state and reduces reliance on the self and the tenets of the American Dream. Programs created by the Great Society continue to face the chopping block with each annual budget drafted by Congress, and many of the ills of the nation are regularly pinned on the legislation passed by the Eighty-Eighth, Eighty-Ninth, and Ninetieth Congresses of the United Stations in the mid-1960s.

As a former member of the House of Representatives and Senate, Johnson had more than three decades of experience with the intricacies and processes of the legislature, as well as a vast network of friends to wheel and deal with to get his pet legislation passed. From his time as a legislator, Johnson could count among his friends Everett Dirksen of Illinois, the minority leader of the Republicans, as well as Hubert Humphrey, the majority whip, who was also an ardent supporter of civil rights. These men were instrumental in passing the legislation Johnson deeply believed in. It didn't hurt that Johnson was also well known to strongly punish those legislators he believed had crossed him.

The Great Society wasn't only about societal and economic improvements, however. Johnson also believed strongly in the preservation of federal funding for arts and cultural programs. The National Foundation on the Arts and the Humanities Act of 1965 created the National Endowment for the Arts (NEA) and the National Endowment for the Humanities (NEH), national art and humanities councils to advise the NEA and NEH, and over time, arts and humanities councils in each state.

In the creation of these two acts, Johnson was likely strongly influenced by the programs of the Works Progress Administration during the Great Depression. These programs, which included the Federal Art Project, Federal Writers Project, and Federal Theater Project, not only gave artists employment in an incredibly difficult economy, they also introduced art to communities that was made by members of the community and funded by the community. Today, some of the strongest criticism of the Great Society is directed at the NEA by conservatives and family groups, who balk at the usage of federal funding for arts and culture. Throughout its history, some of the works of art have often been considered highly controversial and outside the spectrum of good values.

While Congress passed the legislation that encompassed the Great Society, Johnson was increasingly sending more American youth to fight in the escalating conflict in Vietnam. So unpopular with Americans was the US involvement in the Vietnam War that Johnson's hopes of a Great Society were dashed by 1968, and he chose not to run for reelection. Evidence suggests that money that could be spent domestically reducing poverty and uplifting American people in the United States was instead diverted to the war effort. This difficult negotiation in the purchase of "guns and butter"—spending on munitions for the war while simultaneously spending on Americans domestically—is said to have hurt the American economy well into the 1970s, and newly elected Richard Nixon, rather than reducing the war effort, instead reduced the appropriations for American programs created during the Johnson administration.

Perspectives on Modern World History: The Great Society explores the impact of the programs more than fifty years after Johnson took office. It includes chapters on the historical background and controversies of Johnson's body of legislation as well as personal narratives from individuals directly affected by the legislation. Fifty years on, it is astonishing to reflect on where the nation stood in the early 1960s and, due to the influence of the Great Society, where it stands now.

World Map

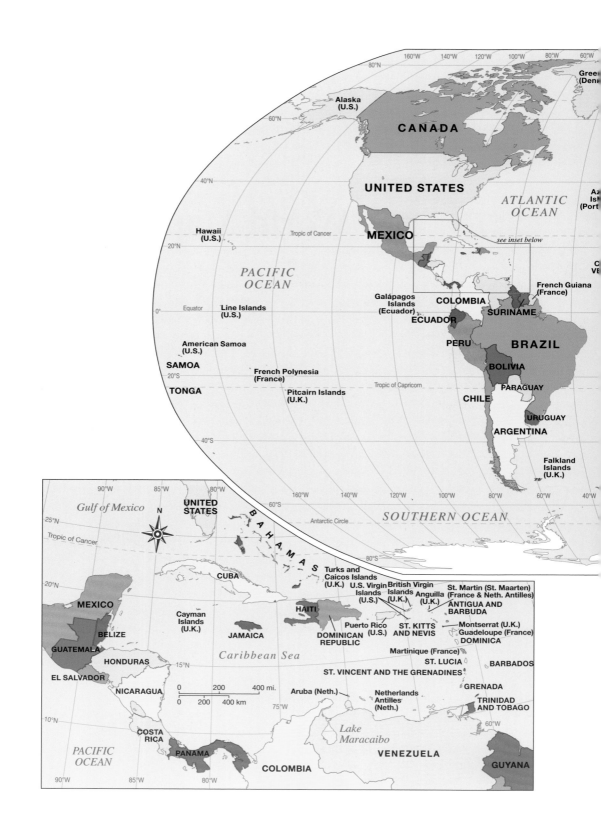

160°W   140°W   120°W   100°W   80°W   60°W

80°N

60°N

Gree
(Den

Alaska
(U.S.)

CANADA

40°N

UNITED STATES

ATLANTIC
OCEAN

A
Is
(Port

20°N

Hawaii
(U.S.)

Tropic of Cancer

MEXICO

see inset below

C
VE

PACIFIC
OCEAN

Galápagos
Islands
(Ecuador)

COLOMBIA

French Guiana
(France)

0°

Equator

Line Islands
(U.S.)

ECUADOR

SURINAME

American Samoa
(U.S.)

PERU

BRAZIL

SAMOA

20°S

French Polynesia
(France)

BOLIVIA

TONGA

Pitcairn Islands
(U.K.)

Tropic of Capricorn

PARAGUAY

CHILE

URUGUAY

40°S

ARGENTINA

Falkland
Islands
(U.K.)

160°W   140°W   120°W   100°W   80°W   60°W   40°W

60°S

SOUTHERN OCEAN

Antarctic Circle

80°S

90°W   85°W   80°W

Gulf of Mexico

N

UNITED
STATES

25°N

Tropic of Cancer

B
A
H
A
M
A
S

Turks and
Caicos Islands
(U.K.)

U.S. Virgin
Islands
(U.S.)

British Virgin
Islands
(U.K.)

Anguilla
(U.K.)

St. Martin (St. Maarten)
(France & Neth. Antilles)

20°N

CUBA

ANTIGUA AND
BARBUDA

MEXICO

Cayman
Islands
(U.K.)

HAITI

Puerto Rico
(U.S.)

ST. KITTS
AND NEVIS

Montserrat (U.K.)
Guadeloupe (France)

JAMAICA

DOMINICAN
REPUBLIC

DOMINICA

BELIZE

Caribbean Sea

Martinique (France)

GUATEMALA

ST. LUCIA

BARBADOS

HONDURAS

15°N

ST. VINCENT AND THE GRENADINES

EL SALVADOR

0   200   400 mi.

Aruba (Neth.)

GRENADA

NICARAGUA

0   200   400 km

Netherlands
Antilles
(Neth.)

TRINIDAD
AND TOBAGO

75°W

60°W

10°N

COSTA
RICA

Lake
Maracaibo

PACIFIC
OCEAN

PANAMA

VENEZUELA

GUYANA

COLOMBIA

90°W   85°W   80°W

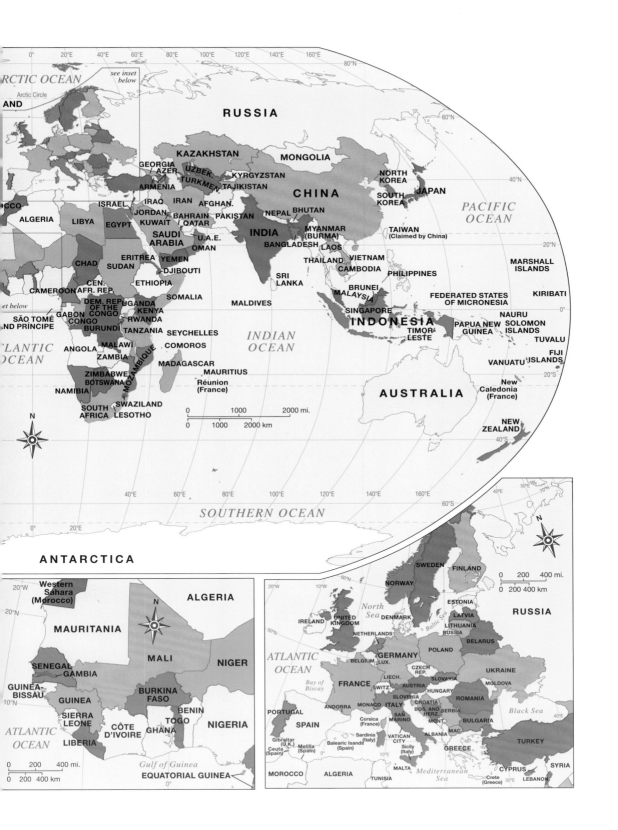

CHAPTER 1

Historical Background on the Great Society

Lyndon B. Johnson's Great Society

Gale Encyclopedia of US Economic History

In the following viewpoint, the editors of a reference resource provide an overview of the Great Society. The term refers to a series of legislative initiatives championed by US president Lyndon B. Johnson (LBJ). The laws aimed to reform US society, in particular the elimination of poverty and racial injustice, and addressed issues in education, medical care, urban challenges, the environment, and transportation. While Johnson's initiatives were initially popular with voters, he lost Americans' support after getting the country involved in an increasingly costly war in Vietnam. Civil unrest and other societal problems across the country seemed to get worse at the same time that billions of dollars were being spent on Great Society initiatives. Opposition to Great Society programs helped Republicans win national elections in the decades following LBJ's administration. Despite criticism and controversies, some Great Society programs continue to enjoy popular support, the authors write, and the debate about the Great Society's legacy continues.

Photo on previous page: US president Lyndon Johnson signs the Immigration and Nationality Act of 1965—one of the many historic laws commonly known as Great Society legislation—on Liberty Island in New York Harbor. (© Everett Collection/Newscom.)

SOURCE. "The Great Society," *Gale Encyclopedia of US Economic History*, 1st ed. Copyright © 1999 Cengage.

The United States mourned when President John F. Kennedy (1960–1963) was assassinated on November 22, 1963. But despite the tragedy, the country was experiencing an era of unprecedented economic health. President Kennedy had already proposed a series of government-funded programs aimed at spreading U.S. prosperity to people still mired in poverty, such as the residents of Appalachia or of the urban ghettoes. When Kennedy's Vice President, Lyndon B. Johnson (1963–1968) assumed the presidency, he pushed to make many of Kennedy's proposals into law. Capitalizing on U.S. stability, as well as the emotions of Kennedy's death, Johnson proposed anti-poverty, civil rights, education, and health care laws. In a speech at the University of Michigan in May 1964, Johnson said he hoped these programs would help create a "Great Society."

> The United States experienced astounding economic growth in the 1950s and 1960s.

Great Society programs, as they came to be known, assisted millions, but they were very controversial. In the short run, funding for these costly programs decreased, as the United States spent more and more fighting the Vietnam War (1964–1975). In the long run, many critics have charged that these initiatives resulted in high taxes, "big government," and that they actually hurt the very people they were designed to help. Nonetheless, Great Society programs such as Medicare, which assists the elderly with medical expenses, remained popular and in the late 1990s they were still a crucial part of many Americans' lives.

Great Society programs were not the first large scale effort by the federal government to aid the disadvantaged. President Franklin D. Roosevelt (1932–1945) promised a "New Deal" to all Americans when he was elected. This "New Deal" was a long list of employment,

income-assistance, and labor legislation, and it also had many critics.

Fulfilling Roosevelt's and Kennedy's Legacies

But President Roosevelt's New Deal came at a time of mass poverty, when the United States and the world were living through the tough economic times of the Great Depression (1929–1939). Having emerged from World War II (1939–1945) as the world's most powerful nation, the United States experienced astounding economic growth in the 1950s and 1960s. Many Americans who barely had enough to eat during the Depression, now found themselves living in brand new homes and driving automobiles.

President Kennedy believed this national wealth could be used to uplift those who had not yet shared

Martin Luther King Jr. (left) and other civil rights leaders meet with President Lyndon Johnson (center) at the White House in 1964. (© Universal History Archive/Getty Images.)

> Johnson challenged Congress to pass the Economic Opportunity Act, the foundation for what came to be known as the "war on poverty."

in the good economic times. Particularly disadvantaged were African Americans, who faced legal segregation in the South and poverty and discrimination in the North. In the tradition of Roosevelt's New Deal, Kennedy proposed employment, education, and health care legislation.

This was the legacy President Lyndon Johnson (1963–1969) hoped to fulfill with his Great Society. A masterful politician, Johnson may have lacked Kennedy's public grace, but he made up for it with political savvy. A former leader in the Senate, Johnson would need these skills to enact his ambitious programs which faced serious opposition in Congress.

The War on Poverty Begins Johnson's Legislative Agenda

During the summer of 1964 Johnson challenged Congress to pass the Economic Opportunity Act, the foundation for what came to be known as the "war on poverty." Johnson also proposed the Civil Rights Act of 1964, which combated racial discrimination. Johnson said enacting these bills would be a fitting tribute to Kennedy.

Johnson's initiatives seemed to be popular with voters. He won the 1964 election in a landslide. Capitalizing on what appeared to be a mandate from the American people, Johnson quickly proposed a wide range of programs for mass transportation, food stamps, immigration, and legal services for the poor. Bills aiding elementary, secondary, and higher education were also passed. Medicaid and Medicare were established to assist the poor and elderly, respectively, with medical treatment.

Other initiatives created the Department of Housing and Urban Development, aimed at improving housing conditions, particularly in crowded cities, and Project

GREAT SOCIETY LEGISLATION

President Lyndon Johnson announced his Great Society program during his State of the Union address in 1964. He outlined a series of domestic programs that he promised would eliminate poverty and inequality in the United States. By the end of Johnson's term, Congress had implemented 226 of 252 of his legislative requests.

Year	Legislation	What It Provided
1964	24th Amendment	Banned poll tax in federal elections.
1964	Civil Rights Act of 1964	Banned discrimination in public accommodations and employment, guaranteed Equal Opportunity in the workplace.
1964	Urban Mass Transportation Act	Provided financial aid for urban mass transit systems.
1964	Economic Opportunity Act	Authorized Head Start, Job Corps, Work-Study program for university students. Volunteers in Service to America (VISTA), Neighborhood Youth Corps, basic education and adult job training, food stamps, and other Community Action Programs (CAPS).
1964	Wilderness Preservation Act	Banned commercial use in more than 9 million acres of national forest.
1965	Medicare	Provided medical aid for people over 65.
1965	Voting Rights Act of 1965	Eliminated previous strategies used to keep minorities and women from voting, including literacy tests. Required that ballots be provided in other languages if requested.
1965	Immigration and Nationality Act of 1965	Abolished the National Origins Formula that had been in place since 1924. The Immigration and Nationality Act of 1965 meant that preference was no longer given to immigrants from Northern European countries. It allowed people from other areas, including Asia and Africa, equal immigration status into the US. It continued to restrict the number of immigrants allowed into the US annually.
1965	Higher Education Act	Provided federal scholarships.
1965	Department of Housing and Urban Development Act	Formed to administer federal housing programs. Commonly referred to as "HUD."
1966	Demonstration Cities and Metropolitan Development Act of 1966	The "Model Cities" program attempted to rehabilitate urban areas that were facing increased violence and poverty by funding improvement projects.
1966	Medicaid	Provided low cost medical insurance to poor Americans.
1966	Truth in Packaging Act	Set standards for labeling consumer products.

Taken from: The Gilder Lehrman Institute of American History, "Study Aid: Great Society Legislation," www.gilderlehr

> Johnson presented [Great Society programs] not only as moral and just but also as a way to further expand the U.S. economy.

Head Start, which aided poor children in their earliest years of education. The National Endowment for the Humanities and the Corporation for Public Broadcasting were created in an effort to expand access to culture.

Budgets and War Create Obstacles

These programs cost billions of dollars but Johnson presented them not only as moral and just but also as a way to further expand the U.S. economy using education, job training, and income assistance. Johnson's party, the Democrats, won big again in the 1966 elections. However, forces were already converging, which would make it difficult to carry out Great Society programs. Across the country cities were exploding with demonstrations and even riots. Some wondered why problems seemed to be getting worse, just as billions of dollars had been committed to solving them.

A more daunting problem lay halfway around the world. The War in Vietnam claimed an increasing amount of Johnson's attention. And the war became just as controversial as Johnson's War on Poverty. It was also becoming more and more expensive as troops and supplies poured into the region to combat the "Viet Cong" guerrilla fighters and the North Vietnamese Army. Johnson was pressured to hike taxes to cover the soaring costs of the war and his Great Society measures. Johnson's need for a tax increase gave political opponents leverage to demand domestic spending cuts. By 1968 Johnson's top economic and political priority was the increasingly unpopular war in Vietnam. This commitment ultimately led to him refusing to seek reelection as the Democratic presidential candidate.

That year also saw California Governor Ronald Reagan (1911–[2004]) fail in his bid to become the Republican presidential candidate. But twelve years later, when the nation's economy was stagnant, Reagan was elected president on a platform that identified many of Johnson's programs as the source of the nation's economic woes. Republicans like Reagan claimed the burden of Great Society initiatives on taxpayers had become too great while poverty only seemed to worsen. "It was 25 years ago that Lyndon Johnson announced his plans for 'The Great Society,'" the conservative magazine *National Review* wrote in 1989. "Today the phrase refers only to a bundle of welfare programs that have helped make the federal budget a chronic problem."

Republicans stepped up their attack into the 1990s and in 1994 they won majorities in both houses of Congress. They continued to criticize federal spending on programs such as Aid to Families with Dependent Children, more commonly called welfare, which were greatly expanded under the Great Society. Some Democrats said the attacks unfairly singled out society's most vulnerable citizens. Republicans argued that such social programs lead to dependency, which creates problems for both the beneficiary and the nation. Even President Bill Clinton (1993–[2001]), a Democrat, declared an "end to welfare as we know it."

Despite the criticism, a diverse selection of Great Society programs, from Medicare to public television, remain politically popular. The ultimate legacy of the Great Society will surely be debated for decades to come.

The Great Society rests on abundance and liberty for all. It demands an end to poverty and racial injustice, to which we are totally committed in our time. But that is just the beginning.

LBJ Describes His Vision for a Better America

Lyndon B. Johnson

Six months into his presidency, Lyndon B. Johnson (LBJ) gave the 1964 commencement speech at the University of Michigan. In the speech, he defines the goals and vision of a Great Society. LBJ explains that the challenge for Americans is not to be satisfied with being a rich or a powerful society, but to use their power and riches to advance civilization. He describes elements of such a society, including the lack of poverty and racial injustice, access to education, and communion with nature. He says that the decay in urban centers must be reversed to turn them into great cities, and the country's natural resources and beauty must be protected. He extols building the Great Society as a moral duty and describes the government's role as "creative federalism," in which the federal authorities support local initiatives and action. Building this new world, he says, will realize the vision and goals of the country's initial settlers. Johnson was the thirty-sixth president of the United States and held the office from 1963 to 1969.

SOURCE. Lyndon Johnson, "Speech at the University of Michigan, May 22, 1964," *Public Papers of the Presidents of the United States: Lyndon B. Johnson, 1963–1964, vol. I.* Washington, DC: Government Printing Office, 1965, pp. 704–707.

It is a great pleasure to be here today [at the University of Michigan on May 22, 1964]. This university has been coeducational since 1870, but I do not believe it was on the basis of your accomplishments that a Detroit high school girl said, "In choosing a college, you first have to decide whether you want a coeducational school or an educational school."

Well, we can find both here at Michigan, although perhaps at different hours.

I came out here today very anxious to meet the Michigan student whose father told a friend of mine that his son's education had been a real value. It stopped his mother from bragging about him.

I have come today from the turmoil of your capital [Washington, DC] to the tranquility of your campus to speak about the future of your country.

The purpose of protecting the life of our Nation and preserving the liberty of our citizens is to pursue the happiness of our people. Our success in that pursuit is the test of our success as a Nation.

> The challenge of the next half century is whether we have the wisdom to use that wealth to enrich and elevate our national life, and to advance the quality of our American civilization.

For a century we labored to settle and to subdue a continent. For half a century we called upon unbounded invention and untiring industry to create an order of plenty for all of our people.

The challenge of the next half century is whether we have the wisdom to use that wealth to enrich and elevate our national life, and to advance the quality of our American civilization.

Your imagination, your initiative, and your indignation will determine whether we build a society where progress is the servant of our needs, or a society where old values and new visions are buried under unbridled growth. For in your time we have the opportunity to

Johnson's Address to Congress After the Kennedy Assassination

An important component of President Lyndon B. Johnson's Great Society legislation was the Civil Rights Act of 1964. Civil rights legislation had been part of his predecessor's political agenda, and Johnson began to push for passage of the act within days of John F. Kennedy's assassination in late 1963. Following are excerpts of Johnson's first address as US president to a joint session of Congress.

All I have I would have given gladly not to be standing here today.

The greatest leader of our time has been struck down by the foulest deed of our time. Today John Fitzgerald Kennedy lives on in the immortal words and works that he left behind. . . . No words are sad enough to express our sense of loss. No words are strong enough to express our determination to continue the forward thrust of America that he began. . . .

This Nation has experienced a profound shock, and in this critical moment, it is our duty, yours and mine, as the Government of the United States, to do away with uncertainty and doubt and delay, and to show that we are capable of decisive action; that from the brutal loss of our leader we will derive not weakness, but strength; that we can and will act and act now. . . .

First, no memorial oration or eulogy could more eloquently honor President Kennedy's memory than the earliest possible passage of the civil rights bill for which he fought so long. We have talked long enough in this country about equal rights. We have talked for one hundred years or more. It is time now to write the next chapter, and to write it in the books of law.

I urge you again, as I did in 1957 and again in 1960, to enact a civil rights law so that we can move forward to eliminate from this Nation every trace of discrimination and oppression that is based upon race or color. There could be no greater source of strength to this Nation both at home and abroad. . . .

Let us here highly resolve that John Fitzgerald Kennedy did not live—or die—in vain. And on this Thanksgiving eve, [let us] gather together to ask the Lord's blessing, and give Him our thanks.

SOURCE. *Lyndon B. Johnson, "Address Before a Joint Session of the Congress, November 27, 1963,"* Public Papers of the Presidents of the United States: Lyndon B. Johnson, 1963–1964, *vol. 1, entry 11, pp. 8–11. Washington, DC: Government Printing Office, 1965.*

move not only toward the rich society and the powerful society, but upward to the Great Society.

The Qualities of a Great Society

The Great Society rests on abundance and liberty for all. It demands an end to poverty and racial injustice, to which we are totally committed in our time. But that is just the beginning.

The Great Society is a place where every child can find knowledge to enrich his mind and to enlarge his talents. It is a place where leisure is a welcome chance to build and reflect, not a feared cause of boredom and restlessness. It is a place where the city of man serves not only the needs of the body and the demands of commerce but the desire for beauty and the hunger for community.

> The Great Society is not a safe harbor, a resting place, a final objective, a finished work.

It is a place where man can renew contact with nature. It is a place which honors creation for its own sake and for what it adds to the understanding of the race. It is a place where men are more concerned with the quality of their goals than the quantity of their goods.

But most of all, the Great Society is not a safe harbor, a resting place, a final objective, a finished work. It is a challenge constantly renewed, beckoning us toward a destiny where the meaning of our lives matches the marvelous products of our labor.

So I want to talk to you today about three places where we begin to build the Great Society—in our cities, in our countryside, and in our classrooms.

Improving American Cities

Many of you will live to see the day, perhaps 50 years from now, when there will be 400 million Americans—four-fifths of them in urban areas. In the remainder of this century urban population will double, city land will double, and we will have to build homes, highways, and facilities equal to all those built since this country was first settled. So in the next 40 years we must rebuild the entire urban United States.

Aristotle said: "Men come together in cities in order to live, but they remain together in order to live the good life." It is harder and harder to live the good life in American cities today.

The catalog of ills is long: there is the decay of the centers and the despoiling of the suburbs. There is not enough housing for our people or transportation for our traffic. Open land is vanishing and old landmarks are violated.

Worst of all expansion is eroding the precious and time honored values of community with neighbors and communion with nature. The loss of these values breeds loneliness and boredom and indifference.

Our society will never be great until our cities are great. Today the frontier of imagination and innovation is inside those cities and not beyond their borders.

New experiments are already going on. It will be the task of your generation to make the American city a place where future generations will come, not only to live but to live the good life.

I understand that if I stayed here tonight I would see that Michigan students are really doing their best to live the good life.

This is the place where the Peace Corps was started. It is inspiring to see how all of you, while you are in this country, are trying so hard to live at the level of the people.

Improving the American Countryside

A second place where we begin to build the Great Society is in our countryside. We have always prided ourselves on being not only America the strong and America the free, but America the beautiful. Today that beauty is in danger. The water we drink, the food we eat, the very air that we breathe, are threatened with pollution. Our parks are overcrowded, our seashores over-burdened. Green fields and dense forests are disappearing.

A few years ago we were greatly concerned about the "Ugly American." Today we must act to prevent an ugly America.

> Our society will not be great until every young mind is set free to scan the farthest reaches of thought and imagination.

For once the battle is lost, once our natural splendor is destroyed, it can never be recaptured. And once man can no longer walk with beauty or wonder at nature his spirit will wither and his sustenance be wasted.

Improving American Classrooms

A third place to build the Great Society is in the class-rooms of America. There your children's lives will be shaped. Our society will not be great until every young mind is set free to scan the farthest reaches of thought and imagination. We are still far from that goal.

Today, 8 million adult Americans, more than the entire population of Michigan, have not finished 5 years of school. Nearly 20 million have not finished 8 years of school. Nearly 54 million—more than one-quarter of all America—have not even finished high school.

Each year more than 100,000 high school graduates, with proved ability, do not enter college because they cannot afford it. And if we cannot educate today's youth, what will we do in 1970 when elementary school enrollment will be 5 million greater than 1960? And high school enrollment will rise by 5 million. College enrollment will increase by more than 3 million.

In many places, classrooms are overcrowded and curricula are outdated. Most of our qualified teachers are underpaid, and many of our paid teachers are unqualified. So we must give every child a place to sit and a teacher to learn from. Poverty must not be a bar to learning, and learning must offer an escape from poverty.

But more classrooms and more teachers are not enough. We must seek an educational system which grows in excellence as it grows in size. This means better training for our teachers. It means preparing youth to enjoy their hours of leisure as well as their hours of labor. It means exploring new techniques of teaching, to find new ways to stimulate the love of learning and the capacity for creation.

Creating Solutions with National and Local Cooperation

These are three of the central issues of the Great Society. While our Government has many programs directed at those issues, I do not pretend that we have the full answer to those problems.

But I do promise this: We are going to assemble the best thought and the broadest knowledge from all over the world to find those answers for America. I intend to establish working groups to prepare a series of White House conferences and meetings—on the cities, on natural beauty, on the quality of education, and on other emerging challenges. And from these meetings and from this inspiration and from these studies we will begin to set our course toward the Great Society.

> You can help build a society where the demands of morality, and the needs of the spirit, can be realized.

The solution to these problems does not rest on a massive program in Washington, nor can it rely solely on the strained resources of local authority. They require us to create new concepts of cooperation, a creative federalism, between the National Capital and the leaders of local communities.

The Generation That Will Lead America into the Future

Woodrow Wilson once wrote: "Every man sent out from his university should be a man of his Nation as well as a man of his time."

Within your lifetime powerful forces, already loosed, will take us toward a way of life beyond the realm of our experience, almost beyond the bounds of our imagination.

For better or for worse, your generation has been appointed by history to deal with those problems and to lead America toward a new age. You have the chance never before afforded to any people in any age. You can help build a society where the demands of morality, and the needs of the spirit, can be realized in the life of the Nation.

President Lyndon Johnson (center foreground) participates in commencement ceremonies at the University of Michigan in May 1964. (© Cecil Stoughton/Corbis.)

So, will you join in the battle to give every citizen the full equality which God enjoins and the law requires, whatever his belief, or race, or the color of his skin?

Will you join in the battle to give every citizen an escape from the crushing weight of poverty?

Will you join in the battle to make it possible for all nations to live in enduring peace—as neighbors and not as mortal enemies?

Will you join in the battle to build the Great Society, to prove that our material progress is only the foundation on which we will build a richer life of mind and spirit?

The Powers to Build a Better Civilization

There are those timid souls who say this battle cannot be won; that we are condemned to a soulless wealth. I do not agree. We have the power to shape the civilization that we want. But we need your will, your labor, your hearts, if we are to build that kind of society.

Those who came to this land sought to build more than just a new country. They sought a new world. So I have come here today to your campus to say that you can make their vision our reality. So let us from this moment begin our work so that in the future men will look back and say: It was then, after a long and weary way, that man turned the exploits of his genius to the full enrichment of his life.

Federal Food Assistance to Millions of Americans Grows from a Small Pilot Program

Food and Nutrition Service, US Department of Agriculture

In the following viewpoint, the US Department of Agriculture provides the history of food stamp programs (FSP) in the United States. The program currently known as Supplemental Nutrition Assistance Program (SNAP) can trace its history to three decades before the Great Society programs of the 1960s, the viewpoint shows. However, it was Lyndon B. Johnson's Food Stamp Act of 1964 that created the first permanent FSP. The viewpoint summarizes major provisions in the law and changes to the FSP over the years, including development in the 1960s, expansion through the 1970s, significant changes in the 1980s, and the current electronic benefit transfer system (EBT). The Food and Nutrition Service of the US Department of

SOURCE. "Supplemental Nutrition Assistance Program (SNAP): A Short History of SNAP," Food and Nutrition Service, US Department of Agriculture, November 20, 2013. www.fns.usda.gov.

Agriculture works to end hunger and obesity and administers fifteen federal nutrition assistance programs, including SNAP; the Special Supplemental Nutrition Program for Women, Infants, and Children (WIC); and school meals.

The idea for the first FSP [food stamp program] is credited to various people, most notably Secretary of Agriculture Henry Wallace and the program's first Administrator Milo Perkins. The program operated by permitting people on relief to buy orange stamps equal to their normal food expenditures; for every $1 worth of orange stamps purchased, 50 cents worth of blue stamps were received. Orange stamps could be used to buy any food; blue stamps could only be used to buy food determined by the Department to be surplus.

Over the course of nearly 4 years, the first FSP reached approximately 20 million people at one time or another in nearly half of the counties in the U.S.—peak participation was 4 million—at a total cost of $262 million. The first recipient was Mabel McFiggin of Rochester, New York; the first retailer to redeem the stamps was Joseph Mutolo; and the first retailer caught violating the program was Nick Salzano in October 1939. The program ended "since the conditions that brought the program into being—unmarketable food surpluses and widespread unemployment—no longer existed."

The Pilot Food Stamp Program

The 18 years between the end of the first FSP and the inception of the next were filled with studies, reports, and legislative proposals. . . . On Sept. 21, 1959, P.L. 86-341 authorized the Secretary of Agriculture to operate a food stamp system through Jan. 31, 1962.

The [Dwight D.] Eisenhower Administration never used the authority. However, in fulfillment of a campaign promise made in West Virginia, President [John F.] Ken-

Food stamp benefits used to be distributed with paper certificates such as these on display at a 2004 event in Illinois. Current recipients get their benefits via electronic card transfers. (© Tim Boyle/Getty Images.)

nedy's first Executive Order called for expanded food distribution and, on Feb. 2, 1961, he announced that food stamp pilot programs would be initiated. The pilot programs would retain the requirement that the food stamps be purchased, but eliminated the concept of special stamps for surplus foods. A Department spokesman indicated the emphasis would be on increasing the consumption of perishables. Isabelle Kelley, who was part of the four-person team that designed the new program, became its first director and the first woman in USDA to head an action program.

> "Mr. and Mrs. Alderson Muncy of Paynesville, West Virginia, were the first food stamp recipients on May 29, 1961."

Mr. and Mrs. Alderson Muncy of Paynesville, West Virginia, were the first food stamp recipients on May 29, 1961. They purchased $95 in food stamps for their 15-person household. In the first food stamp transaction, they bought a can of pork and beans at Henderson's Supermarket. By January 1964, the pilot programs had expanded from eight areas to 43 (40 counties, Detroit, St. Louis, and Pittsburgh) in 22 States with 380,000 participants.

The Food Stamp Act of 1964

On Jan. 31, 1964, President [Lyndon] Johnson requested Congress to pass legislation making the FSP permanent. Secretary Orville Freeman submitted proposed legislation to establish a permanent FSP on April 17, 1964. The bill eventually passed by Congress was H.R. 10222, introduced by Congresswoman [Leonor K.] Sullivan. Among the official purposes of the Food Stamp Act of 1964 were strengthening the agricultural economy and providing improved levels of nutrition among low-income households; however, the practical purpose was to bring the pilot FSP under Congressional control and to enact the regulations into law. The major provisions were:

- the State Plan of Operation requirement and development of eligibility standards by States;
- the requirement that recipients purchase their food stamps, paying an amount commensurate with their normal expenditures for food and receiving an amount of food stamps representing an opportunity more nearly to obtain a low-cost nutritionally adequate diet;
- the eligibility for purchase with food stamps of all items intended for human consumption except alcoholic beverages and imported foods (the House ver-

sion would have prohibited the purchase of soft drinks, luxury foods, and luxury frozen foods);

> In April 1965, participation topped half a million.

- prohibitions against discrimination on bases of race, religious creed, national origin, or political beliefs;

- the division of responsibilities between States (certification and issuance) and the Federal Government (funding of benefits and authorization of retailers and wholesalers), with shared responsibility for funding costs of administration; and

- appropriations for the first year limited to $75 million; for the second year, to $100 million; and, for the third year, to $200 million.

The Department estimated that participation in a national FSP would eventually reach 4 million, at a cost of $360 million annually.

Program Expansion in the 1960s and Early 1970s

In April 1965, participation topped half a million. (Actual participation was 561,261 people.) Participation topped 1 million in March 1966, 2 million in October 1967, 3 million in February 1969, 4 million in February 1970, 5 million one month later in March 1970, 6 million two months later in May 1970, 10 million in February 1971, and 15 million in October 1974. Rapid increases in participation during this period were primarily due to geographic expansion.

The early 1970s were a period of growth in participation; concern about the cost of providing food stamp benefits; and questions about administration, primarily timely certification. It was during this time that the issue was framed that would dominate food stamp legislation ever after: How to balance program access with program accountability? . . .

The Food Stamp Act of 1977

Both the outgoing Republican Administration and the new Democratic Administration offered Congress proposed legislation to reform the FSP in 1977. The Republican bill stressed targeting benefits to the neediest, simplifying administration, and tightening controls on the program; the Democratic bill focused on increasing access to those most in need and simplifying and streamlining a complicated and cumbersome process that delayed benefit delivery as well as reducing errors, and curbing abuse. . . . Amidst all the themes, the one that became the rallying cry for FSP reform was "EPR"— eliminate the purchase requirement—because of the barrier to participation the purchase requirement represented. The bill that became the law—S. 275—did eliminate the purchase requirement. . . .

> Recognition of the severe domestic hunger problem in the latter half of the 1980s led to incremental improvements.

The integrity provisions of the new program included fraud disqualifications, enhanced Federal funding for States' anti-fraud activities, and financial incentives for low error rates.

EPR was implemented Jan. 1, 1979. Participation that month increased 1.5 million over the preceding month. . . .

The large and expensive FSP came under close scrutiny of both the Executive Branch and Congress in the early 1980s. Major legislation in 1981 and 1982 enacted cutbacks. . . .

Program Improvements in the Mid- to Late 1980s

Recognition of the severe domestic hunger problem in the latter half of the 1980s led to incremental improvements in the FSP in 1985 and 1987, such as elimination of sales tax on food stamp purchases, reinstitution of categorical eligibility, increased resource limit for most households ($2,000), eligibility for the homeless, and expanded nutrition education. The Hunger Prevention Act of 1988 and the Mickey Leland Memorial Domestic Hunger Relief Act in 1990 foretold the improvements that would be coming. The 1988 and 1990 legislation accomplished the following:

- increasing benefits by applying a multiplication factor to Thrifty Food Plan costs;
- making outreach an optional activity for States;
- excluding advance earned income tax credits as income;
- simplifying procedures for calculating medical deductions;
- instituting periodic adjustments of the minimum benefit;
- authorizing nutrition education grants;
- establishing severe penalties for violations by individuals or participating firms; and
- establishing EBT as an issuance alternative. . . .

The Current Era: EBT

Electronic Benefit Transfer (EBT) is an electronic system that allows a recipient to authorize transfer of their government benefits from a Federal account to a retailer account to pay for products received. EBT is used in all 50 States, the District of Columbia, Puerto Rico, the Virgin Islands, and Guam. State food stamp agencies work with contractors to procure their own EBT systems for delivery of Food Stamp and other state-administered benefit programs.

In EBT systems, food stamp recipients apply for their benefits in the usual way, by filling out a form at their local food stamp office. Once eligibility and level of benefits have been determined, an account is established in the participant's name, and food stamp benefits are deposited electronically in the account each month. A plastic card, similar to a bank card, is issued and a personal identification number (PIN) is assigned or chosen by the recipient to give access to the account. Recipients are offered the opportunity to change the PIN number at any time, and are offered ongoing training if they have any problems accessing the system.

EBT eliminates the cumbersome processes required by the paper food stamp system. By eliminating paper coupons which could be lost, sold, or stolen, EBT may help cut back on food stamp fraud. EBT creates an electronic record of each food stamp transaction, making it easier to identify and document instances where food benefits are exchanged for cash, drugs, or other illegal goods.

All States are using EBT as an alternative for SNAP issuance and, in some cases, for other programs such as USDA's Special Supplemental Nutrition Program for Women, Infants and Children (WIC); and the Temporary Assistance to Needy Families (TANF) program, the Federal block-grant program operated by the Department of Health and Human Services. As of July 2004, all 50 States, the District of Columbia, the Virgin Islands, and Guam operated state-wide, city-wide, and territory-wide EBT systems to issue SNAP benefits.

LBJ Melts Some Butter to Provide More Guns

Hobart Rowen

The following viewpoint is a newspaper article from 1968, a year in which escalating war costs and a slowing economy forced US president Lyndon B. Johnson to reduce the federal budget for social programs. The author writes that the administration cut civilian spending, which indicated a sharp deceleration of progress on Great Society programs. The president's tone was grim as he spoke of the need to make tough choices, the author writes. More telling may be the fact that the budget did not use the phrase "Great Society" at all. The author analyzes the proposed budget and finds that it had dramatic departures from what was previously anticipated; he believes this under-scored the great cost of the Vietnam War. Hobart Rowen was an economics and business columnist for the *Washington Post* and served as the paper's financial editor from 1966 to 1975.

E ver since the major escalation of the Vietnam war in mid-1965, President Johnson has been insistent that the Nation could have both "guns and butter." It has been this dogged pursuit, basically, that fed Congressional resistance to his proposals for a tax increase.

But his new budget, sent to Congress yesterday, melts down much of the butter. For the first time, the President established "priorities" in the face of the mounting bill for Vietnam, which he put at more than $75 billion for the 4 fiscal years 1966 through 1969.

It is more than coincidence that the strongest call for re-ordering budgetary priorities has come from Chairman Wilbur Mills (D-Ark.) of the House Ways and Means Committee, who until now has frustrated the Administration's efforts to raise taxes.

> The tone is grim, and the budget message starts right in with the need for making 'difficult choices.'

Last Oct. 6 [1967], for example, Mills said the real issue between him and the Administration was the need for "basic changes in Federal programs." He urged "a pause in the head-long rush toward ever bigger government."

Mr. Johnson appears to have gotten the message. The new budget cuts civilian spending and future programs. If it doesn't mark the final demise of the Great Society, it registers a sharp deceleration in its progress.

Two years ago, in delivering the fiscal 1967 budget, the President said: "we are a rich nation and can afford to make progress at home while meeting obligations abroad . . . For this reason, I have not halted progress in the new and vital Great Society programs in order to finance the costs of our efforts in Southeast Asia."

The Tone Is Grim

Last year at this time, the President sidetracked mention of the Great Society, but said that "in our domestic programs, we will continue to press ahead, at a controlled and reasoned pace."

This year the tone is grim, and the budget message starts right in with the need for making "difficult choices." The "stubborn foes" of poverty at home are listed along with the challenge "of an obstinate foe" abroad.

But not only is the phrase "Great Society" absent, there is not even a separate grouping of the programs as such.

Asked by a reporter at the annual budget press conference what he would "recommend" as a compilation "for what used to be called Great Society program," outgoing Budget Director Charles L. Schultze grimaced and said: "I can't answer that question."

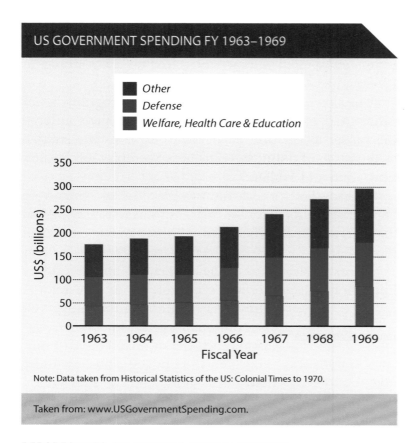

US GOVERNMENT SPENDING FY 1963–1969

Other
Defense
Welfare, Health Care & Education

US$ (billions)

Fiscal Year

Note: Data taken from Historical Statistics of the US: Colonial Times to 1970.

Taken from: www.USGovernmentSpending.com.

But an examination of tables in the budget message shows that major education, health, welfare, labor, urban development, and housing programs are allotted $20.8 billion for fiscal 1969, an increase of only $1.7 billion or 9 percent.

In fiscal 1968, the same programs had been moved up by $3.9 billion to $19.1 billion, or a boost of 25 percent.

Education Suffers Most

Making allowance for Medicare expenditures, which some might include in a Great Society definition, the story is the same.

If Medicare payments, which come out of trust fund operations, are included in a Great Society definition, the new budget would show a 10 percent increase in the coming year, compared to a 30 percent jump in the current fiscal year. Medicare payments in fiscal 1969 were estimated at $5.8 billion, compared to $5.1 billion in 1968 and $3.4 billion in 1976.

The slowdown in expansion of social programs is not distributed equally. Education programs have suffered the most—a fact that insiders say explains the sudden resignation of John W. Gardner, Secretary of Health, Education and Welfare.

Total outlays for education are placed at $4.7 billion—a bare $200 million over last year. But this tells only part of the story, since the President withheld major chunks of money already authorized by Congress.

For example, Title 1 of the Elementary and Secondary Education Act authorized expenditures of $2.6 billion. Only $1.2 billion is in the budget. Of $1 billion authorized for higher education facilities, a miniscule $75 million is in the budget. Thus, on those two items alone, almost $2.4 billion in authorized education monies has been held back.

> "There are dramatic exceptions that underscored the cost of the war in Vietnam.

Health Expenditures

By and large, authorizations for health expenditures came off better, although there are dramatic exceptions that underscored the cost of the war in Vietnam.

Thus, of $90 million authorized for air pollution, only $30 million is to be spent this year, and $60 million is withheld. And of $195 million for new health research facilities, only $8 million is in the budget, and $186 million held back.

A separate budget tally called "federal aid to the poor," which overlaps the Great Society grouping outlined above, places the 1969 figure at $27.7 billion, compared with $24.6 billion in 1968 and $21.1 billion in 1967. But more than half—$15.9 billion—will come from well-established Social Security and public assistance programs.

Women protest the Vietnam War and ongoing social injustice in the United States—competing priorities for the Lyndon Johnson presidency—at a protest in front of the US Capitol in January 1968. (© **AP Photo.**)

The imprint of the war and the President's new order of priorities does not impinge exclusively on the Great Society. While allotting small increases "to the most urgent needs of our Nation today," he set out a list of "program" cutbacks or deferrals totaling $2.9 billion in other civilian programs, of which $1 billion will be reflected in actual expenditure cuts this coming year.

Proposed Retrenchments

Among these proposed retrenchments—most of which will require Congressional approval—are slashes of $197 million in agriculture programs; $156 million in ship construction; $224 million in college facility grants; $61 million in Interior Department programs; $447 million in space programs; and $40 million in business loans.

If Congress approves, such savings will be spread over several budget years.

There are other reflections of the President's reluctant concession that "we cannot do everything we would wish to do." They show up not as programs or expenditure cutbacks, but less-than-planned increases.

'It is not the rise in regular budget outlays which requires a tax increase, but the cost of Vietnam.'

For example, the supersonic airliner program is allowed an increase of $250 million in outlays for fiscal 1969, well below what is required for the target completion date of 1974.

A revealing tally in the budget shows that Vietnam spending is now equal to 3 percent of the Gross National Product, and that all other Federal activities (outside of social insurance trust funds) amounts to only 13.9 percent, well under the 16 percent average of 1958–60.

Observing this declining trend in non-Vietnam spending, the President said: "it is not the rise in regular budget outlays which requires a tax increase, but the cost of Vietnam."

It may be recalled that last year the President refused to tie his tax request so directly to the Vietnam adventure, a reluctance that many experts think weakened his case on the Hill.

But now there is a new approach, as Treasury Secretary Henry H. Fowler made almost plaintively clear: "Many wanted us to restrict new programs," he told a press conference. "This has been done. They wanted us to cut back existing programs this year—this has been done."

Whether the "austerity" so displayed will get the President his desired tax increase remains to be seen. But he has gone at least part of the way to meet the demands for Federal retrenchment.

CHAPTER 2

Controversies Surrounding Great Society Programs

Despite Missteps, the Great Society Helped Americans

Bill Moyers

In the following viewpoint, the press secretary for President Lyndon B. Johnson (LBJ) discusses the legacy of the Great Society. Writing twenty years after LBJ's presidency, the author describes how the president's political priorities were aligned with the nation's economic prosperity. This confluence allowed the nation to tackle poverty and other social problems without raising taxes and to build a healthy economy for the baby boom generation. The author also describes some of the challenges posed by racial integration and the existing political structure. According to the author, the Vietnam War eroded the national consensus about LBJ's grand vision, and the president lost the support he needed to complete the unfinished business of the Great Society. The author lists many benefits enjoyed by Americans because of the Great Society, while also conceding that its reach may have exceeded its grasp. Journalist and

Photo on previous page: Martin Luther King Jr. (center) and other civil rights leaders participate in the Selma to Montgomery, Alabama, marches of 1965 in support of voting rights. President Lyndon Johnson considered the Voting Rights Act of 1965 among the greatest achievements of his Great Society legislation. (© **Robert Abbott Sengstacke/Getty Images.**)

SOURCE. Bill Moyers, "Second Thoughts: Reflections on the Great Society," *New Perspectives Quarterly*, Winter 1987. Copyright © 1987 by New Perspectives Quarterly. Reproduced with permission of Blackwell Publishing Ltd.

commentator Bill Moyers has had a long and distinguished career in print and broadcast media, public television in particular. He served as the White House press secretary from 1965 to 1967.

"This is the time to act," Lyndon Johnson [LBJ] said on the first morning after that fateful day of John Kennedy's assassination in 1963. By nightfall of that same day he instructed his chief economic advisor to proceed full steam ahead on planning the anti-poverty program. Within days, he met with the leaders of every major civil rights organization in the country and he called the powers in Congress.

On the map of his mind there was already appearing, in bold relief, the routes he would ask the country to follow. Our resources were growing at a rate of 5 percent a year and his economic advisors, in the words of Walter Heller, assured him that, "in our time, the engine of our economy would be the mightiest engine of human progress the world has ever seen." Just by shifting a small portion of the additional resources created by growth, it was thought we could abolish poverty without raising taxes. Lyndon Johnson came to believe we could all join in the positive sum game of getting richer together.

> [Johnson] approved an antipoverty program that would try to end-run some deeply ingrained institutional obstacles to social justice.

The economics matched the politics. Critics attacked his notion of consensus, but the President kept insisting that, in politics, you cast your stakes wide and haul up a big tent with room for everybody who wants in. He sought to stimulate the private sector into generating growth and jobs. The budgetary deficit, the growth rate of the money supply and, in the beginning, the ratio of social to defense spending were all moderately increased to promote growth. I am one of those who think it worked. We know now that, with the soaring birthrates of the baby-boom, the American workforce increased an extraordinary 40% between 1965 to 1980. In no small part due to the economic and social policies of the Johnson years, the number of jobs almost doubled in the postwar period. We can fairly ask, what might have happened had the crowded baby-boom generation arrived in the workforce without those jobs?

Seeking Equality for All

If the President shared the liberal faith that by enlarging the size of the economic pie every one would gain, he instinctively sensed it wasn't enough. He said if income

President Lyndon Johnson shakes hands with an Appalachian resident in 1964. Johnson sought to help people in impoverished areas of the United States with federal programs. (© Everett Collection/Newscom.)

grew without change in relative shares, there would be no increase in equality. He believed equality was the moving horizon which America had been chasing for all its history.

So, with no popular mandate except the conviction that what the best and wisest parents want for their child, the community should want for all its children, he approved an antipoverty program that would try to end-run some deeply ingrained institutional obstacles to social justice.

In his more expansive moments, LBJ talked of going all the way. "Let's conquer the vastness of space, create schools and jobs for everyone," he said. "Let's care for the elderly, let's build schools and libraries, let's increase the affluence of the middle-class. Let's improve the productivity of business, let's do more for civil rights in one Congress than the last one hundred years combined. Let's get started in all of these areas," as he said in his first State of the Union Address, "by summer" and "with no increase in spending."

The Challenges of Racial Integration

We were in Tennessee. During a motorcade, the President spotted some ugly racial epithets scrawled on signs by a few plain, he called them homely, white women on the edge of the crowd. Late that night in the hotel, long past midnight, he was still going on about how poor whites and poor blacks had been kept apart so that they could separately be fleeced. "I'll tell you what's at the bottom of it," he said. "If you can convince the lowest white man that he's better than the best colored man, he won't notice you're picking his pocket. Hell, give him somebody to look down on, and he'll even empty his pockets for you."

For weeks in 1964 the President carried in his pocket the summary of a census bureau report showing that the lifetime earnings of an average black college graduate

Major Features of the Civil Rights Act of 1964

Title I—Voting Rights: Banned different voter registration requirements by race.

Title II—Public Accommodations: Outlawed discrimination based on race, color, religion, or national origin in public accommodations, such as establishments that provide lodging to transient guests (hotels, motels, inns); facilities principally engaged in selling food for consumption on the premises (restaurants, cafeterias, soda fountains); and places of exhibition or entertainment (theaters, concert halls, sports arenas).

Title III—Desegregation of Public Facilities: Prohibited state and local governments from denying access to public facilities on the basis of race, religion, gender, or ethnicity.

Title IV—Desegregation of Public Education: Encouraged the desegregation of public schools and authorized the US Attorney General to file suits to enforce school desegregation.

Title V—Civil Rights Commission: Broadened the powers, rules, and duties of the US Commission on Civil Rights (established in 1957), and extended it through 1968.

Title VI—Nondiscrimination in Federally Assisted Programs: Prohibited discrimination on the basis of race, color, or national origin by any recipient of federal funds (organizations, companies, schools, government agencies, etc.); authorized the withdrawal of federal funds from discriminatory programs.

Title VII—Equal Employment Opportunity: Outlawed employment discrimination based on race, color, religion, sex, or national origin; created the Equal Employment Opportunity Commission to review discrimination complaints.

Title VIII—Registration and Voting Statistics: Required the Census Bureau to collect registration and voting statistics of race, color, and national origin.

Title IX—Intervention and Removal of Cases: Enabled civil rights cases to be moved to federal high courts from unfriendly district or state courts, and authorized US Attorney General intervention in civil rights suits.

Title X—Community Relations Service: Created the Community Relations Service to help communities in resolving disputes related to discrimination based on race, color, or national origin.

> "America was a segregated country when LBJ came to power. It wasn't when he left."

were actually lower than that of a white man with an eighth-grade education. And when the *New York Times* reported in November 1964 that racial segregation was increasing instead of decreasing, he took his felt tip pen and scribbled across it, "Shame, shame, shame," and sent it to Everett Dirksen, the Republican leader of the Senate.

In those days our faith was in integration. Lyndon Johnson thought the opposite of integration was not just segregation, but disintegration—a nation unravelling.

America was a segregated country when LBJ came to power. It wasn't when he left. From his very first hours in office, he would move to combat it on a broad front. But he also knew not an inch would be won cheaply. The Civil Rights Act of 1964 is to many of us a watershed in American history. It was one of the most exhilarating triumphs of the Johnson years. Yet, late on the night of signing the bill, I found the President in a melancholy mood. I asked what was troubling him. "I think we just delivered the South to the Republican Party for a long time to come," he said. Even as his own popularity soared in that heady year, the President saw the gathering storm of a backlash.

Addressing the Power Structure

In 1965, I sent to the President an essay by Herbert Marcuse, the leftist philosopher so admired by the student movement, in which Marcuse applauded LBJ's objectives, but doubted the government's ability to stay the course. "Rebuilding the cities, restoring the countryside, redeeming the poor and reforming education," said Marcuse, "could produce nondestructive full employment. This requires," he said, "nothing more, nothing less than the actual reconstruction outlined in the President's program. But the very program," he said, "requires the transformation of power structures standing in the way of its fulfillment."

An example of this was the call I got from Chicago's Mayor Richard Daley. Almost before I could say, hello, he said, "What in the hell are you people doing? Does the President know he's putting money in the hands of subversives?" Mayor Daley's definition of a subversive was anyone outside of his political machine. And, through the Community Action Program of the antipoverty program, the President was pouring money, "M-O-N-E-Y," Mr. Daley spelled it out on the phone, "money to poor people that aren't part of our organization. Didn't the President know they'd take that money to bring him down?" In the end, as I found out, the Community Action Director eventually hired for Chicago was one of Richard Daley's own men. So, Chicago was made safe for poverty and democracy.

The Vietnam War Rouses the Opposition

"We can continue the Great Society while we fight in Vietnam," he told the country. To the President, both were the unfinished business of his generation.

This proved an improvident and deadly combination and contributed to the erosion of his cherished consensus into strenuous and sometimes violent conflict.

Such conflicts, ranging from the problems with Mayor Daley or [Alabama governor] George Wallace to the race riots in our major cities, would have been serious enough without the Vietnam War. But, an unpopular war caused defections on the part of people who might otherwise have supported the domestic vision. Opponents of the war and critics of the Great Society were soon finding one another's company against a government they saw as a common foe; and the more the President sought to drive dissent to the fringe of the public square, the more the square blazed with the fires of his own effigies. By

1967, neither the President nor the country talked any more of a grand vision.

What Worked and What Failed

In 1967, 75% of all Americans over 65 had no medical insurance and a third of the elderly lived in poverty. More than 90% of all black adults in the South were not registered to vote. Across the nation, there were only about 200 black elected officials. There was no Head Start for kids.

> Some things that went wrong were blamed on this Great Society without cause.

Today, Medicare, food stamps, and more generous Social Security benefits have helped reduce poverty among the elderly by half. Nearly 6,000 blacks hold elected office. A majority of small children attend preschool programs. The bedrock of the Great Society—Medicare, Medicaid, federal aid to education, the right of blacks to citizenship—are permanent features of the American system.

What went wrong? Some things that went wrong were blamed on this Great Society without cause. As [writer and TV commentator] Ben Wattenberg has pointed out, there was no "Soft-On-Crime Act" of 1966. There was no "Permissive Curriculum Act" of 1967, or a "Get Vindictive with Business Act" of 1968. But plenty of things went wrong. Progress fell victim to pork-barrel politics. The idea of giving the poor resources for leadership never got the support it deserved. Employment training projects suffered from high drop-out rates. There were often no jobs when the training ended. And, of course, the costs exceeded the estimate.

We had, in short, jumped too fast, spread out too far, too thinly over too vast a terrain. And then we gave to war on a distant front [Vietnam] against an enemy that would not bargain, compromise or reason. They wanted only to win.

Intrusive Great Society Programs Hurt the US Economy and Its People

Ronald Reagan

In the following viewpoint, US president Ronald Reagan says that Great Society programs and ideology hurt the US economy and describes the benefits of his administration's approach. The Founding Fathers, he says, warned against excessive government. He traces the economic problems of the late 1970s and 1980s, particularly high unemployment rates, to the years of government expansion triggered by the Great Society. The War on Poverty harmed rather than helped the poor because they suffer most in a weak economy, he reasons. In contrast, his administration's efforts to reduce government improved the economy and lowered taxes in just a couple of years. He also argues that individuals and free institutions are the principal means of social and economic progress, not a government with utopian ideals. Reagan was the fortieth president of the United States, serving from 1981 to 1989.

SOURCE. Ronald Reagan, "Remarks at a Fundraising Dinner Honoring Former Representative John M. Ashbrook in Ashland, Ohio," Ronald Reagan Presidential Library and Museum, May 9, 1983.

Fom their own harsh experience with intrusive, overbearing government, the Founding Fathers made a great breakthrough in political under- standing: They understood that it is the excesses of government, the will to power of one man over another, that has been a principle source of injustice and human suffering through the ages. The Founding Fathers under- stood that only by making government the servant, not the master, only by positing sovereignty in the people and not the state can we hope to protect freedom and see the political commonwealth prosper.

In 1776 the source of government excess was the crown's abuse of power and its attempt to suffocate the colonists with its overbearing demands. In our own day, the danger of too much state power has taken a subtler but no less dangerous form. Out of the best of inten- tions, government has intervened in areas where it is neither competent nor needed nor wanted by the mass of Americans.

Federal Spending and the 1980s Recession

There is no better example of the wisdom of limited gov- ernment and the price paid by societies that forgot that wisdom than the economic problems we've encountered in recent years. The notion that government planners could fine-tune the economy from Washington led to a vicious cycle of boom and bust, periods of high inflation followed by periods of high unemployment. . . .

Now, all of us hope, of course, that the unemployment situation will ease much more quickly than current [early 1980s] predictions suggest. But if past recessions were the rule, unemployment will remain a lagging indicator in an otherwise brightening economy so the unemployed will be among the last to feel the benefits of the recovery. But those who have for so long preached the benefits of bigger government should be asked to acknowledge that the economic conditions that led to recession and unemployment were created by years of growth in government and the climate of government expansion and interference.

> The government was draining off America's productivity and placing an enormous drag on the economy.

When this administration took office, Federal spending had tripled in the preceding 10 years and taxes had doubled in the preceding 5 years. The national debt was hitting a trillion dollars—social spending had quadrupled in one decade. The budget for the Department of Health and Human Services became the third largest entity in the world, just behind the national budgets of the United States and the Soviet Union. One social program, food stamps, had grown from a $70 million experimental program in 1965 to an $11 billion program in 1981—an incredible 16,000-percent increase.

The government was draining off America's productivity and placing an enormous drag on the economy. Higher and higher taxes and inflation were discouraging work, risk, and the willingness of business and labor to invest time or money in economic expansion.

The Great Society Did More Harm than Good

Now this tremendous slowdown in the economy was more than a statistical event. It hurt those who could least afford to be hurt. Particularly hard hit were those traditionally lower income groups that make up such a high percentage of the unemployed. Minimum wage laws—with no allocation made or allowance made for young people doing marginal work—kept many young people from gaining the entry-level positions that mean invaluable job training and eventually full-time careers.

Or take the slowdown in economic progress made by those with low incomes. As pointed out in a recent article by Charles Murray in the *Public Interest* magazine, the great expansion of government programs that took place under the aegis of the Great Society coincided with an end to economic progress for America's poor people. From 1949 until just before the Great Society got underway in 1964, the percentage of American families in poverty fell dramatically—from nearly 33 percent to only 18 percent. But by 1980, with the full impact of the Great Society's programs being felt, the trend had reversed itself, and there was an even higher proportion of people living in poverty than in 1969.

> The great social spending schemes failed for the vast majority of poor Americans.

The simple truth is that low inflation and economic expansion in the years prior to the Great Society meant enormous social and economic progress for the poor of America. But after the gigantic increases in government spending and taxation, that economic progress slowed dramatically. If we had maintained the economic progress made from 1950 through 1965, black family income in 1980 would have been nearly $3,000 higher than it was.

The great social spending schemes failed for the vast majority of poor Americans. They remain trapped in economic conditions no better than those of a decade-and-a-half ago. The poverty programs failed precisely because they grew without regard for the burden they and other social programs were imposing on the overall economy. As social spending multiplied, economic growth slowed, and the economy became less and less able to generate the jobs and incomes needed to lift the poor out of poverty, not to mention the fact that inflation stimulated by government growth hit the poor the hardest, especially by devaluating the payments of those on welfare.

The growth of government programs did little for the poor; they were sometimes even counterproduc-

The First African American President Renews the War on Poverty

As . . . the country commemorates the 50th anniversary of President Lyndon Johnson's "War on Poverty" [in January 2014] President Barack Obama . . . praised Johnson's crusade as an "economic and moral mission" that helped "each and every American fulfill his or her basic hopes". Through jobs and education, new opportunities were created, and access to health care for seniors, the poor, and people with disabilities were expanded, Obama said.

But today's Democrat in the White House also warned the nation that Johnson's "War on Poverty" was not something merely for history books. "As every American knows, our works is far from over", Obama said.

"In the richest nation on Earth, far too many children are still born into poverty, far too few have a fair shot to escape it, and Americans of all races and backgrounds experi-ence wages and incomes that aren't rising, making it harder to share in the opportunities a growing economy provides", Obama said.

Instead, the President said, America must redouble the efforts to make sure the US economy works for every working citizen. "It means helping our businesses create new jobs with stronger wages and benefits, expanding access to education and health care, rebuilding those communities on the outskirts of hope, and constructing new ladders of opportunity for our people to climb."

Obama [also designated] troubled neighborhoods in five cities and areas as "Promise Zones", eligible for tax breaks and other forms of assistance designed to create jobs and improve education, housing and public safety.

SOURCE. *"The Torch Has Passed: Obama Takes Over War on Poverty,"* Euronews, *January 8, 2014. www .euronews.com.*

tive. From 1965 to '74, for example, the Federal Urban Renewal program spent more than $7 billion and ended a total failure, destroying more housing units than it replaced. The Federal regulations and grants of the Model Cities program in the late 1960's spent more than

$2\frac{1}{2}$ billion and didn't halt urban decay. But all of these programs—while they did fund jobs for an army of Federal bureaucrats and consultants—put a huge burden on the productive sector of the American society. It was the working people who had to pay the taxes, carry the burden of inflation, and get thrown out of work when the inevitable economic slowdown occurred.

Helping the Economy by Reducing Government

Today, because of our attempts to restrict and cut back on government expansion and to retarget aid toward those most in need, and away from those who can manage without Federal help, the working people of America are directly benefiting. We have brought inflation down from . . . double-digit levels. And now for the last 6 months, it has been less than one-half of 1 percent. . . .

For a family on a fixed income of $20,000, the improvement in inflation has meant about $1,700 more in purchasing power. And because of our tax program, a median-income family of four in 1983 will pay $700 less in Federal income taxes. And if they try to do anything about that third tax cut, I sleep with a veto pen under my pillow.

But beyond all this, however, cutting back on government intrusions into the marketplace and its drain on the economy has meant the beginning of a solid recovery.

Auto production is up 40 percent in the first quarter over the same time a year ago. And in March, new home sales were up over 50 percent, building permits were up more than 70 percent, and building starts were up by 75 percent over the same time last year. Consumer confidence has had its best monthly gain in 9 years, all the way to 77 percent as measured by the Conference Board. We now have the lowest prime interest rate in 4 years; inflation is better than the double-digit figures of a few years ago; and the stock market is healthy again.

And this need not be a temporary recovery. If we can continue to cut the growth in spending, if we can continue to hold the line on taxes, consumer and business confidence will remain high, and the recovery will be sustained over a long period of time. Once again, America's working people will know that hard work, saving, and sound investment will pay off for them and their children in the future. And this will mean far more to the lower income groups that have been so badly hit by unemployment and inflation than all the government programs of the past. It'll mean economic growth and expanding opportunity over a long period of time. Instead of having government trying to redistribute a shrinking economic pie, that pie will be expanding, and everyone will have a chance at a larger share.

> We must resist that well-intentioned statism of those who urge even more spending and higher taxes.

The Dangers of Big Government

But if we're to continue this progress, we must resist that well-intentioned statism of those who urge even more spending and higher taxes. The British political philosopher, Michael Oakeshott, has warned us about the dangers of government that tries to do too much:

> To some people, government appears as a vast reservoir of power which inspires them to dream of what use might be made of it. They have favorite projects of various dimensions which they sincerely believe are for the benefit of mankind. They are thus disposed to recognize government—an instrument of passion, the art of politics to enflame and direct desire.

Well, here, I would submit, is the central political error of our time. Instead of seeing the people and their free institutions as the principal means of social and economic progress, our political opposition has looked at

US president Ronald Reagan holds a copy of his proposals for welfare reform titled "Up from Dependency" at a February 1987 event. (© Dirck Halstead/The LIFE Images Collection/Getty Images.)

government and bureaucracy as the primary vehicle of social change. And this marked the onslaught of special interest politics, the notion that every noble social goal is the business of government, that every pressure group has its claim on the tax dollars of working people, that national legislation means brokering and bartering with the largest share going to the most powerful of the noisiest political constituency.

This is the antithesis of fair government, of democratic rule, and orderly government. As Mr. Oakeshott has observed, it is the conjunction of utopian dreaming and government power that degenerates into tyranny. Even beyond the raids on the national treasury, the huge deficits, the high inflation and taxation—the very abuses that brought down so many empires and nations in the past—this trend toward well-intentioned but overwhelming government also diminishes personal freedom and the autonomy of those branches of government closest to the people.

Even two centuries ago, the Founding Fathers understood this. They anticipated the danger. John Adams wrote that government tends to run every contingency into an excuse for enhancing power in government. And Thomas Jefferson put it more directly when he predicted happiness for America but only "if we can prevent the government from wasting the labors of the people, under the pretense of taking care of them. . . ."

Limited Government Enables Progress

Now, some, of course, mistake this to mean the negation of government. Far to the contrary, it is by clearly restricting the duties of government that we make government efficient and responsive. By preventing government from overextending itself we stop it from disturbing that intricate but orderly pattern of private transactions among various institutions and individuals who have different social and economic goals. In short, like the Founding Fathers, we recognize the people as sovereign and the source of our social progress. We recognize government's role in that progress, but only under sharply defined and limited conditions. We remain aware of government's urge to seek more power, to disturb the social ecology and disrupt the bonds of cooperation and interchange among private individuals and institutions through unnecessary intrusion or expansion.

When new management takes over a failing business or a coach tries to revitalize a sports team, both will frequently find that the key to success is cutting out the extraneous or extravagant, while returning to basics and emphasizing those resources that have been traditionally successful. Well, this is precisely what we're trying to do to the bloated Federal Government today: remove it from interfering in areas where it doesn't belong, but at the same time strengthen its ability to perform its constitutional and legitimate functions.

Great Society Programs Are Fiscally and Morally Irresponsible

Robert W. Patterson

In the following viewpoint, the author makes the case that the United States has two types of social safety net programs. On the one hand are the New Deal-type programs, which he explains are good for the federal budget and support sound moral values. Great Society programs, on the other hand, are a drain on the economy and support countercultural and immoral values. He explains that it is unhelpful to think of programs with roots in the New Deal, such as Social Security and Medicare, as "entitlements" because they are self-financing and require that the beneficiaries pay into the program. Programs with roots in the Great Society, however, are means-tested, meaning that they are granted based on the individual's financial means. These programs have increased the federal deficit to unsustainable levels and need drastic reform, he writes. Robert W.

SOURCE. Robert W. Patterson, "Don't Blame New-Deal Entitlements: The Great-Society Welfare State and the Fiscal Crisis," *The Family in America*, vol. 25, no. 3, Summer 2011. Copyright © 2011 by The Howard Center for Family, Religion and Society. All rights reserved. Reproduced by permission.

Patterson is the editor of *The Family in America: A Journal of Public Policy* and teaches political rhetoric and speechwriting at Patrick Henry College in Purcellville, Virginia. His writing has appeared in publications such as *National Review Online*, the *Weekly Standard*, and *Christianity Today*.

Much of the current preoccupation with "entitlements" as the main driver of federal deficits is misguided. As Byron York, chief political correspondent for the *Washington Examiner* has noted, the blowout budgets of President [Barack] Obama—which have driven federal spending to 25 percent of GDP and created budget shortfalls of around $1.4 trillion for each of the last three years—have absolutely nothing to do with Social Security and Medicare. While the journalist concedes that these "entitlements need to be controlled in the long run," he nonetheless claims, "today's deficit crisis is not one of entitlements. It was created by out-of-control spending on everything other than entitlements." That is the understated reality, especially if by entitlements York means federal social-insurance programs—e.g., Social Security and Medicare—sustained by payroll deductions from American workers anticipating future benefits for themselves and their families. In the case of Medicare, the program is also supported by premiums paid by current retirees. That important qualifier of funding by payroll deductions and premiums is often forgotten by politicians, media analysts, and average citizens, all of whom persist in regarding Medicaid—the state-run, "means-tested" welfare program that has no financing mechanism—also as an entitlement.

Indeed, the two pay-as-you-go entitlements, Social Security and Medicare, are actually budget bracers, not budget busters. According to data published in the annual reports of the Social Security and Medicare Board of Trustees, these self-financing programs have each

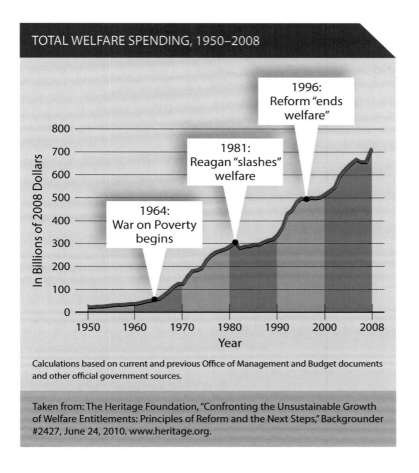

TOTAL WELFARE SPENDING, 1950–2008

1996:
Reform "ends
welfare"

1981:
Reagan "slashes"
welfare

1964:
War on Poverty
begins

Calculations based on current and previous Office of Management and Budget documents
and other official government sources.

Taken from: The Heritage Foundation, "Confronting the Unsustainable Growth
of Welfare Entitlements: Principles of Reform and the Next Steps," Backgrounder
#2427, June 24, 2010. www.heritage.org.

been running annual surpluses for years. The two sister
entitlements generated surpluses of $121 billion in 2009
and $32 billion in 2010.

These surpluses are no fluke. Except for a few
years in the late 1970s and early 1980s, these popular
social-insurance programs have been net contributors
to the federal budget going back at least to 1965, when
Medicare was instituted. Annual reports of the Board of
Trustees make it clear that revenue from payroll taxes,
self-employment taxes, income taxes on benefits, and
Medicare premiums have generated combined surpluses
in the four related programs: Old-Age and Survivors

Insurance and Disability Insurance (the two Social Security programs) and Hospital Insurance and Supplemental Medical Insurance (the two Medicare programs). Even as Social Security and Medicare spending has increased dramatically over the years, relative to GDP, so has Social Security and Medicare income. . . . Social Security by itself has since 1996 generated a cumulative revenue surplus of 28 percent, relative to its outgo, raking in more than $9.6 trillion in revenues while paying out $7.5 trillion, or a cumulative surplus of $2.1 trillion.

To be certain, the surpluses will ultimately dry up and become deficits, due to declining marriage rates and anemic birth rates, demographic realities influenced by misguided public policy and court decisions of the 1970s, and realities rarely acknowledged by those who advance entitlement reform, save in the pages of this journal [*The Family in America*]. . . . Real reform requires a recovery of the explicit family orientation that graced the signature New-Deal program. But reforms to correct long-term imbalances of social-insurance trust funds will not resolve the crisis at hand nor help the congressional supercommittee find savings in the federal budget.

> By far the biggest single driver of federal deficits is spending on the means-tested anti-poverty initiatives that have roots in the Great Society of the 1960s.

Means-Tested Programs Drive the Budget Deficit

By far the biggest single driver of federal deficits is spending on the means-tested anti-poverty initiatives that have roots in the Great Society of the 1960s, not New-Deal entitlements traceable to the 1930s. The former include well-known assistance programs such as Medicaid, the Children's Health Insurance Program (SCHIP), Temporary Assistance for Needy Families (TANF), the Low-Income Heat and Energy Assistance Program (LIHEAP), and food stamps, now called the Supplemental Nutrition Assistance Program (SNAP). But that short list does not do justice to the extent and pervasiveness of the U.S. welfare system that has grown astronomically since President Lyndon B. Johnson declared his War on Poverty in 1964. As Peter Ferrara of the Carleson Center for Public Policy warns, the federal-state welfare complex is a "vast empire bigger than the entire budgets of almost every other country in the world," representing 185 overlapping and duplicative initiatives providing "cradle-to-grave services." Another scholar, Robert Rector of the Heritage Foundation, counts "over 70 interrelated means-tested programs" funded

> through four independent agencies and nine federal departments: Health and Human Services, Agriculture, Housing and Urban Development, Labor, Treasury, Commerce, Energy, Interior, and Education. Altogether these programs provide cash, food, housing, medical care, social services, job training, community development funds, and targeted education aid to low-income persons and communities.

The extensive research of Rector, who perhaps knows more about welfare spending than anyone else in Washington, highlights two points: 1) the reversal, since 1989, of the moderating trend in means-tested welfare outlays that characterized the [President Ronald] Reagan years and 2) the escalation of that twenty-year spending spur since President Obama took office, representing, in his words, "a permanent expansion of the welfare state, not a temporary response to the current recession." Regarding the first point, Rector and his colleagues claim that total annual means-tested anti-poverty spending at both federal and state levels has grown faster than

> "The Social Security system is deeply rooted in the social conservatism of the New Deal."

any other category of government spending, including entitlement spending, increasing by nearly 300 percent between 1989 and 2008:

> Means-tested spending on cash, food, and housing increased more rapidly (196 percent) than Social Security (174 percent). The growth in means-tested medical spending [Medicaid] (448 percent) exceeded the growth in Medicare (376 percent). The growth in means-tested aid greatly exceeded the growth in government spending on education (143 percent) and defense (126 percent).

Now, the senior fellow's second point: President Obama not only immediately boosted welfare outlays from $522 billion to $697 billion between 2008 and 2010 but also shifted its twenty-year growth trajectory into a higher gear. Rector calculates that between 2010 and 2019, federal welfare spending will hit $7.8 trillion in current dollars; if state spending is included, the total is $10.8 trillion. Those figures do not include the pending expansion of Medicaid, the single most expensive means-tested assistance program, once President Obama's signature health-care legislation of 2010, popularly known as ObamaCare, kicks in. . . .

Separating the New Deal from the Great Society

These numbers provide empirical reasons for policymakers to give higher priority to retreating from the War on Poverty than from cutting New-Deal entitlements, the latter of which are self-financing and have little to do with current budget deficits. Nor are these fiscal realities the only reason why policymakers need a clear exit strategy for this other war of LBJ, which has become more of a quagmire than Vietnam ever was. Policies that scale back LBJ's misguided social interventions would also resonate with President Ronald Reagan—who, when faced with a budget crisis thirty years ago—chose to go after the means-tested welfare expenditures of the Great Society. As he wrote in his diary in January 1982, after being pummeled by the news media throughout his inaugural year for trying to curtail federal spending, "The press is trying to paint me as trying to undo the New Deal. I'm trying to undo the Great Society."

Reagan's dislike of the legacy of the Great Society is understandable. The differences separating Great-Society initiatives like Medicaid from New-Deal programs like Social Security and Medicare are stark, and have grown even more striking as the society that has emerged from the former stands more and more in contrast to America at mid-twentieth century. For starters, the Social Security system is deeply rooted in the social conservatism of the New Deal, as Allan Carlson has documented. It upholds without apology the child-rich, married parent family as the social and economic ideal; its benefit structure presumes marriage as a vital economic partnership, provides assistance to widowed mothers, and recognizes the economic contribution of full-time mothers who do the unheralded work of rearing the next generation. When coupled with other New Deal-era policies—like the "family wage," as well as income-tax relief for married parents with dependent children—Social Security helped the United States to solve, in the words of French writer R.L. Bruckberger, the perennial "social problem"—the "bitter, obdurate antagonism between rich and poor"— and create a humane economy that became the envy of the world after the Second World War. Indeed, when later linked to Medicare, Social Security spearheaded the family benefits package that the private sector emulated after World War II and which workers today still covet.

In contrast, the social-engineering programs of the Great Society represent everything the New Deal was not. Unlike the limited social insurance programs of the New Deal, the ever-proliferating liberal welfare schemes of the War on Poverty lack the critical ingredient that social-policy scholar Lawrence Mead calls *reciprocity*. To this very day, Social Security and Medicare retain this concept; beneficiaries receive no assistance unless they, or their spouse or parents, have paid into the system for a defined period of time, while benefits are determined in part by their contributions and number of dependents. Accordingly, while Medicare was not adopted until 1965 (and might, therefore, be viewed as a Great-Society program), it remains the only front of the War on Poverty that can be claimed as a legitimate heir of the New Deal; it embodies the reciprocity concept. True, its benefit structure is not as tied to prior contributions as is Social Security's (presenting an opportunity for reform that few policymakers have noticed), but at least Medicare beneficiaries must have paid into the system during their working years and pay premiums in retirement.

> The vices of Great-Society programs transcend fiscal measurements.

Means-Tested Programs and Family Fragmentation

Not so with every other weapon of LBJ's domestic war. From housing to cash welfare, from Head Start to Medicaid, and from job training to food stamps, nearly every handout program of the Great Society is means-tested. Although TANF has imposed modest work requirements and time limits for many, although not all, recipients, the concept of reciprocity or mutuality is considered a dirty word in the Great Society; *dependency* is the governing principle. Consequently, none of Rector's 70 or Ferrara's 185 programs have built-in funding mechanisms. They simply drain both federal and state budgets. As their recipients have never paid into the system, these programs should never be considered "mandatory entitlements" but rather as discretionary experiments subject to downsizing.

Yet the vices of Great-Society programs transcend fiscal measurements. As Myron Magnet of the Manhattan Institute has acutely noted, the War on Poverty embodied some of the worst features of the counterculture of the 1960s. At the same time that the Civil Rights Act of 1964 was opening up new levels of opportunity for racial minorities, the counterculture ridiculed the very virtues that those at the lower end of the income distribution needed to succeed while it celebrated behavior that would keep them from moving into the middle class. Consequently, by subsidizing single motherhood among those who could least afford it, the welfare programs of the Great Society displaced marriage and fathers from low-income families, a staggering loss for the country. These effects of the welfare system persist to this day, even in the wake of the 1996 reform legislation that created TANF. In essence, the welfare policies of the Great Society have eaten away at the very social and economic fabric that the New Deal had explicitly strengthened, especially the married-parent family. Forty-seven years later, welfare dependency among the American citizenry is more extensive than ever, and the poor are far less capable of self-reliance.

Researchers at the liberal Brookings Institution as well as the conservative Heritage Foundation tend to agree on the family fragmentation that arose as the Great Society unfolded, even though they use different reference points. Isabel Sawhill of Brookings claims that "virtually all of the increase in child poverty in the United States since 1970" can be attributed to family breakdown, particularly the growth of single-parent families. With her colleague Ron Haskins, Sawhill has estimated that if U.S. marriage rates had remained unchanged since 1970, child poverty in 2001 would have been reduced by more than 25 percent.

That's a very conservative estimate. In a 2003 study, Rector and his colleagues at Heritage claim that child

> It is difficult to deny that higher levels of government social outlays have gone hand-in-hand with higher levels of family dissolution.

poverty in 2001 would be reduced by more than 80 percent if marriage rates had remained what they were in 1960. In a more recent paper, Rector connects the dots even further, claiming that mushrooming welfare expenditures created the very poverty that it was supposed to alleviate: "The disappearance of marriage in low-income communities is the predominant cause of child poverty in the U.S. today."

The Marriage-Welfare Hypothesis

While not all scholars, especially those committed to growing the welfare state, would agree with Rector's assessment of the exact relationship between welfare, the decline of marriage, and poverty, it is difficult to deny that higher levels of government social outlays have gone hand-in-hand with higher levels of family dissolution. This is not to say that there is no place for means-tested programs, only that the more generous the benefits—and the more relaxed the qualifications to receive means-tested assistance—the greater the downward pressure on marriage rates and the upward pressure on unwed birthrates, consequences that boost demand for the perpetual expansion of the welfare state. . . .

The Imperative of Cutting Welfare Spending

This damage to the social sector, damage evident in the decline in the net marriage rate from which the country has yet to recover, provides another reason for policymakers to reduce means-tested welfare outlays. Just as John Mueller has proposed limiting federal outlays on Social Security and Medicare to a certain percentage of national income to prevent further declines in American fertility, federal outlays for welfare spending likewise ought to be limited to perhaps no more than 3 percent of GDP, just under the level when [President] Bill Clinton left office, to help prevent further declines in marriage and family formation. If that represents too steep of a challenge, Robert Rector's proposed welfare-spending cap that would repeal President Obama's welfare-spending increases offers another option, saving nearly $200 billion a year from current projections.

Policymakers, however, ought to also consider Peter Ferrara's bold call for returning all welfare programs back to the states, as they were before President Johnson beat the drums for his War on Poverty, through block grants "apportioned among the states utilizing current federal funding formulas to the extent possible." Key to Ferrara's proposal reflects a Reagan principle: giving the states the freedom to devise their welfare systems the way they—not the federal government or the welfare establishment—think will best meet the needs and circumstances of their particular state. The only federal directives that would continue to have force in Ferrara's plan are those specifying that funds be used to assist the truly poor, that funds be used without discrimination in accordance with civil-rights law, and that assistance embody reciprocity: given in return for work by the able-bodied. . . .

Policymakers would be foolish to allow tactical disagreements to block the imperative of scaling back means-tested welfare spending relative to GDP. Nor should they allow the current preoccupation with "entitlement reform" to obscure the truly disastrous fiscal consequences of LBJ's Great-Society programs that—unlike FDR's New Deal—deserve blame for bringing America to the brink of insolvency. But in following in the footsteps of President Reagan, policymakers have every reason to retreat, now more than ever, from the former with its pernicious social and budget-busting effects.

A Defense of Great Society Programs Must Account for Demographic Changes

Henry J. Aaron

In the following viewpoint, a health-care policy expert and for-mer federal official writes that the social safety net programs of the 1960s—also known as Great Society programs—were wonderful advances that improved lives for Americans. However, he argues that to save the solemn promise of the programs, they should be reformed. He explains that the federal budget crisis has been caused by higher unemployment rates, tax cuts, and increases in military spending. Cuts to Social Security, Medicare, and Medicaid may be inevitable, the author says. However, he proposes that cuts may be designed to cause the least harm and also to advance other worthwhile objectives. Because people are living longer, he contends, retirement pro-grams should be reformed to encourage people to work until

SOURCE. Henry J. Aaron, "Progressives and the Safety Net," *Democracy*, vol. 27, Winter 2013. Copyright © 2013 by Democracy: A Journal of Ideas. All rights reserved. Reproduced by permission.

they're older. Henry J. Aaron is a senior fellow at the Brookings Institution, a think tank in Washington, DC, and he focuses on the reform of health-care financing, public systems, and tax and budget policy. He was assistant secretary for planning and evaluation at the US Department of Health, Education, and Welfare from 1997 to 1998 and chaired the advisory council on Social Security in 1999.

S omething wonderful happened in the United States during the middle third of the twentieth century. After decades of policies that smacked of Social Darwinism, our country created a strong, if incomplete, social-insurance safety net. The actions our government took expressed a solemn promise to vulnerable Americans. Social Security and Medicare assured the elderly and disabled basic cash income and health care roughly similar to that enjoyed by the rest of the population. They lifted the elderly and disabled from a status of privation to near equality with the nonelderly in both money income and access to health care. Various other federal programs provided food, housing, and educational support, or encouraged their provision by state and local governments. By official measures, poverty among the elderly fell below that of other age groups thanks to Social Security, and health coverage improved markedly for the nonelderly poor because of Medicaid.

> In the second decade of the twenty-first century, [Great Society] advances are under attack and [their] solemn promise is in jeopardy.

Now, in the second decade of the twenty-first century, these advances are under attack and that solemn promise is in jeopardy. To be sure, these programs enjoy enormous popularity. At the same time, however, a solid minority has never accepted the idea that taxes should be used to pay for pensions and health insurance. As long

A sign supporting Social Security benefits is held up in front of the White House during an April 2013 protest against changes to the program. (© Kevin G. Hall/ MCT via Getty Images.)

as economic growth generated enough revenue to pay for these programs and the rest of government's commitments, opponents of social insurance and other elements of the safety net gained little political traction. Three deficit reduction plans enacted during the presidencies of George H.W. Bush and Bill Clinton, along with sustained economic growth, produced budget surpluses in the late 1990s and early 2000s.

But then everything changed, and the national debt ballooned. The recessions of 2001 and 2007–2009 led to higher unemployment and lower revenues. Imprudent tax cuts slashed revenues still more. Wars in Iraq and Afghanistan following the tragedy of 9/11 led to huge increases in military spending. As a result, large and seemingly limitless deficits emerged, and budgetary angst has become epidemic.

In addition, official projections have warned that retiring baby boomers and rapidly rising health-care costs will cause Social Security and Medicare benefits to greatly outpace program revenues. Although these *long-term* forces have little to do with *current* budget deficits, they have combined to generate a sense of fiscal crisis. . . .

A Fabricated "Entitlement Crisis"

Against this backdrop, the American public is being told that the cause of looming financial catastrophe is an "entitlement crisis." Fiscal Jeremiahs [pessimists] warn that the only way to deal effectively with *current* deficits is to cut back Social Security, Medicare, and Medicaid years in the future. The full House of Representatives has twice passed budget plans, crafted by Budget Committee Chairman Paul Ryan, that would replace Medicare with a voucher that beneficiaries could use to buy either private insurance or a plan like traditional Medicare. The Ryan plan would also convert Medicaid into a block grant at spending levels well below what is projected under current law. The grants would not increase during recessions when Medicaid enrollments tend to spike. States, pinched by falling revenues and rising service demands, would have to cut benefits just when they are most needed.

But while reports of a crisis are overblown, and conservative proposals to solve it are draconian, progressives do need to think about how best to reform the entitlement

> "Cuts in Social Security, Medicare, and Medicaid benefits are neither necessary nor desirable and should be resisted."

programs. The simple fact is that Social Security, Medicare, and Medicaid form a very large and growing part of the federal budget—currently 50 percent of noninterest spending. Furthermore, the phrase "entitlement crisis" has been repeated so often and so earnestly that denying its reality is more likely to damage one's own credibility than to dislodge what is actually profound confusion. Cuts in Social Security, Medicare, and Medicaid benefits are neither necessary nor desirable and should be resisted, even as reform of the whole health-care delivery system proceeds. But political and economic realities—the need to secure majority support for measures to lower deficits once economic recovery is well advanced—make some cuts highly likely. It behooves supporters of social insurance to have in reserve program cuts that would do the least harm and might advance other meritorious objectives. To begin this search, one should start with the underlying economic and demographic forces that are driving spending.

Demographics and Entitlements

Three demographic facts are key. Longevity is increasing. In contrast to the past, when life expectancy increased due mostly to declining mortality rates among infants and the young, almost all current and future longevity gains will occur among the old. Large groups of Americans are not sharing in these longevity gains.

Life expectancy has risen throughout most of the industrial era. But the character of that increase has changed profoundly, as documented by Stanford health economists Karen Eggleston and Victor Fuchs in the *Journal of Economic Perspectives*. For most of history, high infant and early-childhood mortality meant that most babies didn't live to grow old or even to child-bearing age. Only 40 percent of babies born in 1900 lived to age 65. Mortality before child-bearing age explains why high birth rates led to little or no population growth. In the early and mid-twentieth century, that changed. Major public health and medical advances—notably, improved sanitation and diet, and antibiotics—caused mortality from infectious diseases to plummet. Now, more than 80 percent of babies are expected to live to age 65.

As mortality rates for young adults approach zero, most longevity gains have to occur among the old. As Eggleston and Fuchs show, that is just what has been happening. The share of longevity gains among those over age 65 has risen from one-fifth at the start of the twentieth century to 80 percent now, and the share is rising.

Uneven Gains in Mortality Rates

For the past couple of decades, these gains have been unequally shared. Research by University of Illinois at Chicago public health professor S. Jay Olshansky and his co-authors documents that most longevity gains have accrued to the well educated. Those with little education are actually dying *younger* than they were in the past. A pre-existing longevity gap is expanding with alarming speed. Between 1990 and 2008, life expectancy at age 25 among white men and women with less than a high-school education *fell* 3.3 years and 5.3 years, respectively. Part of the reason for this drop may well be that those with less-than-high-school education rank lower on the socioeconomic scale now than they did even two decades ago, but much of the shift is a mystery. Among white men and women with at least a college education, life expectancy at age 25 *rose* 4.7 years and 3.3 years, respectively, over that period. In 1990, life expectancy at age 25 for white men with at least a college education was five years more than it was for those with less than a high-school education; by 2008, the gap was 13.1 years.

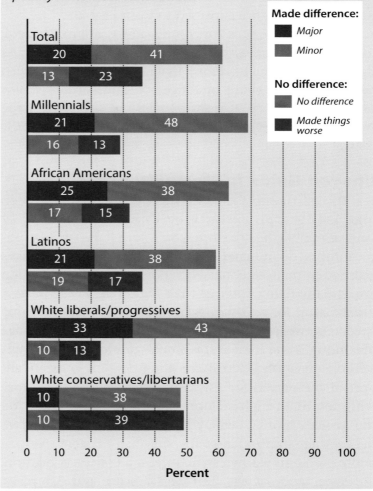

US PUBLIC OPINION ON THE IMPACT OF THE WAR ON POVERTY, 2014

Looking back, would you say the War on Poverty has made a major difference in reducing poverty, made a minor difference in reducing poverty, has made no difference, or has actually made poverty worse in the United States?

Made difference:
- ■ Major
- ■ Minor

No difference:
- ■ No difference
- ■ Made things worse

Total
- 20 | 41
- 13 | 23

Millennials
- 21 | 48
- 16 | 13

African Americans
- 25 | 38
- 17 | 15

Latinos
- 21 | 38
- 19 | 17

White liberals/progressives
- 33 | 43
- 10 | 13

White conservatives/libertarians
- 10 | 38
- 10 | 39

Percent (0 10 20 30 40 50 60 70 80 90 100)

Taken from: Half in Ten Education Fund and the Center for American Progress, "50 Years After LBJ's War on Poverty: A Study of American Attitudes About Work, Economic Opportunity, and the Social Safety Net," January 2014. www .halfinten.org.

For white women, the gap shot up from 1.9 years to 10.5 years.

Even at age 65, the relative gaps remain jarringly large. In 2008, for example, white men with a college education or more had life expectancies five years, or 35 percent, longer than those without a high-school education.

As is well known, whites on average live longer than do blacks. That gap has narrowed somewhat over the last two decades. For reasons that are not well understood, Hispanics have longer life expectancies than either non-Hispanic whites or blacks.

Life Expectancy and Public Policy

While differences among groups are important, so too are averages. Half of men are out of the labor force by age 64, half of women by age 62. On average in 2008, life expectancy for 20 year olds was an additional 59 years, or to age 79. That would mean that the average American works 42 or 44 years and is retired for 15 or 17 years (though in reality, most people are not in the labor force all the time). Crunch all these statistics together and you find that, on average, people typically spend roughly one-third of their adult lives in retirement if one accounts for time spent out of the labor force for child-bearing, for education after age 20, and in unemployment. If consumption is spread evenly over the adult life cycle, roughly one-third of lifetime consumption will occur in retirement.

Stanford economist John Shoven points out that most people live as couples. That changes the arithmetic. Males usually marry women somewhat younger and who have somewhat longer life expectancies than themselves. Shoven points out that roughly 30 years will elapse, on average, before both members of a couple consisting of a 62-year-old man married to a 60-year-old woman will die. Typically, they will have worked no more than 40 years. Shoven bluntly asserts, "You can't finance 30-year retirements with 40-year careers without saving behavior that is distinctly un-American." Whether one uses my arithmetic or Shoven's starker version, it is surely fair to ask whether people will be willing to divert from current consumption enough to both support ever-lengthening retirements and pay for the rest of what they want government to do.

Perhaps they will. After all, workers retire earlier in many other developed countries and receive pensions more generous than those in the United States, even though their life expectancies equal or exceed our own. Still, the reaction of U.S. elected officials to current and projected budget deficits suggests that the United States will not readily accept European-level taxes. Europeans are, to be sure, cutting back pension commitments, but they are doing so from levels much higher than those in the United States and facing elderly populations that, relative to total populations, are considerably larger than any anticipated in the United States. The Republican Party wants no tax increases whatsoever. Even most Democrats support permanent extension of most Bush-era tax cuts.

> "Supporters of the current social-insurance system . . . must think about changes . . . that reduce spending in the least damaging ways and that may accomplish other goals."

Encouraging Later Retirement

For this reason, supporters of the current social-insurance system—even as they fight against any cuts at all—must think about changes in Social Security, Medicare, and other elements of the social safety net that reduce spending in the least damaging ways and that may accomplish other goals. Prominent among such goals should be measures to put in place financial incentives to "nudge" those who can do so without undue hardship to work until later ages than they now do. . . .

Longer working lives mean a larger labor force. A larger labor force means higher output at full employment. And higher output means increased tax collections from individuals and businesses, as well as some reduction in government spending. In a Brookings Institution study (carried out in collaboration with the Urban Institute and Moody's Econometrics and sponsored by the Sloan Foundation), Gary Burtless and I find that if labor force participation among workers over age 55 continues to increase at the same rate observed since 1995, rather than at the slower rate of increase projected by the Social Security Administration, cumulative government revenues would rise $2.7 trillion over the next three decades, mostly from income and payroll taxes, and spending would fall about $600 billion, mostly from Medicare and Social Security savings.

Defending the Safety Net by Reforming It

For several decades support for the legislative landmarks of the New Deal, the Fair Deal [domestic policy reforms under President Harry S. Truman], and the Great Society seemed impregnable, both in the general public and among political elites. Public affection for Social Security and Medicare remains deep and broad. But budget deficits and specific projections for Social Security and Medicare have created a widespread, if misguided, sense that we just can't go on without retrenchment.

The first line of defense should be to defend the importance of these programs and others that comprise the social safety net, and to show that they can be sustained without unduly high tax burdens. But failure to plan for what to do if some ground must be given would be an abdication of responsibility.

For supporters of social insurance, not to make such plans would leave to those programs' critics and enemies the job of designing changes that may prove inescapable.

That is not an outcome that progressives should allow. Nor should progressives deny the very real imperative resulting from a steady increase in longevity: People who can do so should be encouraged to work until later ages than has been common in the past.

The Economic Opportunity Act Built the Infrastructure for Social Service Nonprofits

Rick Cohen

In the following viewpoint, an expert on nonprofit organizations writes that the Great Society's Equal Opportunity Act (EOA) built the infrastructure for social service organizations in the United States. He writes that many of the organizations and services that are now taken for granted, such as early childhood education, legal services for the poor, and community clinics, are a direct result of EOA policies and programs. He reviews the history of partisan attacks against the EOA and its policies, writing that the legislation was not the massive budgetary commitment that some allege. He describes main components of EOA's activities and talks about how each made an enduring contribution to American society. Furthermore, he argues, advocating for social justice must be a part of social service work for it to succeed. Rick Cohen is a national correspondent for *Nonprofit Quarterly* magazine and a former executive director of the National Committee for Responsive Philanthropy. He is an author of three books and publishes the monthly *Cohen Report* newsletter.

Born in 1964, the Economic Opportunity Act (EOA) came into being just as the oldest Baby Boomers were graduating from high school and the first Generation X'ers were toddling around in diapers. In a way, the Economic Opportunity Act is the connective glue of these two generations of nonprofit leaders and nonprofit organizations, at least those believing in and committed to social and economic equity. Despite the "points of light" image of a nonprofit sector driven by individual charitably minded volunteers and donors, much of today's human-service nonprofit infrastructure owes its existence to its Great Society parentage in the EOA.

The [President Lyndon] Johnson Administration's War on Poverty was largely launched through the Economic Opportunity Act legislation. The EOA encountered staunch opposition from entrenched interests inside and outside of government from the very beginning, whittling the program down over the years. For those of us boomers who were products of the War on Poverty, we remember the strange travails of the EOA and the Office of Economic Opportunity that it created. Sometimes it seems amazing how much of the program infrastructure survives, though various programs have endured near-death experiences at the hands of Republican and Democratic overseers.

> The [Economic Opportunity Act] legislation was hardly the massive commitment of funds that critics have alleged.

Partisan Attacks Against the EOA

We remember an amendment proposed in 1970 or 1971 by Congressman John Brademas (D-Indiana) that would have created or expanded child care services for women on welfare, enabling them to go to school or take jobs. At the time, respected conservative pundit James J. Kirkpatrick published a broadside against the program declaring it "Soviet" and that it aimed to "mold U.S. children." Of course, other conservatives were not quite so averse to the program's socialistic tendencies. In fact, [President] Ronald Reagan somehow singled out the EOA-created Head Start program as a piece of the legislation that he would have supported and continued, although his administration tried to limit kids' Head Start participation to one year.

Or how about the 1969 Congressional amendments aimed at weakening the Act? President [Richard] Nixon's anti-poverty chief, a much younger Donald Rumsfeld, defended the EOA, claiming that the legislation would "cripple" the Office of Economic Opportunity [OEO]— even though as a Congressman, Rumsfeld had voted against the Economic Opportunity Act. Who would have ever thought that Rumsfeld would migrate from anti-poverty work to directing the U.S. invasion of Iraq? On Rumsfeld's OEO staff was a young Dick Cheney. Later, as a five-term Republican Congressman from Wyoming, Cheney voted against Head Start appropriations, though in 2000 he said he felt differently about this key EOA program component and would have voted for it.

The EOA legislation President Johnson signed contained less than $1 billion for the nation's anti-poverty efforts. The legislation was hardly the massive commitment of funds that critics have alleged, and the funding that was needed to truly succeed in a war against poverty was sapped by the demands of the nation's other focus at the time, the rapidly increasing commitment to an unwinnable war in Indochina. But from that relatively small financial investment, the Economic Opportunity Act left the nonprofit sector with some of its most essential programmatic and organizational infrastructure:

VISTA (Volunteers in Service to America)

This program was reportedly President Johnson's favorite of all of his anti-poverty initiatives. He told the first 20 VISTA workers, "Your pay will be low; the conditions of your labor often will be difficult. But you will have the satisfaction of leading a great national effort and you will have the ultimate reward which comes to those who serve their fellow man."

Some experts trace the growth of the modern nonprofit sector to the civil rights movement and the legislation and court decisions that led to "the right to pursue legal causes through nonprofit activity and advocacy" as it was put [in] a report by the Association for Research in Nonprofit Organization and Voluntary Action. Although the current descriptions of VISTA on the website of the Corporation for National and Community Service make it seem like it was something of a forerunner of AmeriCorps and its generic community-service stipended-volunteerism approach, VISTA was formulated and operationalized at its outset as an organizing effort aimed at redressing social and economic inequities. In its first year, 2,000 VISTA workers were on the ground in Appalachian coal mining hollows, California migrant labor camps, and inner-city Hartford neighborhoods. Before being stripped of its core function by the [President Bill] Clinton and [President George H.W.] Bush I administrations, VISTA possessed an advocacy orientation that reflected the lessons of the civil rights movement, in particular the recognition that community organizing was required to buck entrenched political and economic interests that wanted to preserve the status quo.

This was not a theoretical matter. In June 1964, before VISTA's actual start-up in 1965, three "Freedom

Summer" civil rights workers—James Chaney, Michael Schwerner, and Andrew Goodman—were viciously beaten and murdered in Nashoba County, Mississippi. Within weeks, President Johnson signed the Civil Rights Act of 1964, and one month later, the Economic Opportunity Act. For some of us of that era, it is hard to match up today's emasculated AmeriCorps VISTA service program with the VISTA that followed on the heels of a defining moment of the civil rights movement.

There are now more than 170,000 VISTA "alumni" bringing their anti-poverty organizing and advocacy experience to the nonprofit, government, and for-profit sectors. The Corporation for National and Community Service says that there are currently 6,500 VISTA "members" working on 1,200 projects across the nation. . . .

Head Start

Despite the recent debates over the flurry of research results suggesting that the long term effects of Head Start are not hugely robust (see the 2010 Head Start Impact Study by the HHS Administration for Children and Families for some mixed results), there are millions of low-income families who swear by Head Start and what it has meant to their children and their families. More than 1,590 agencies are Head Start grantees, ranging in size from small single-site centers to multiple-site programs in large cities. It's hard to imagine how few people don't know about Head Start—or how many people wish their kids could participate in Head Start programs. But do people remember that Head Start started in 1965 as an eight-week summer program for kids who were going to start public school that fall?

> Just about all Gen X'ers and Millennials have been affected by Head Start.

Originally thought of as a "Kiddie Corps" or "Baby Corps," Head Start was much more than a preschool program for poor families. In addition to education, Head Start offered medical care, dental care, and mental-health care even during that first summer of operations, serving 561,000 children on a national budget of $96.4 million. More than 27 million children have passed through Head Start programs since that time. Roughly 900,000 have been enrolled annually since 2000.

Just about all Gen X'ers and Millennials have been affected by Head Start—but most don't know it. In 1968, Head Start provided funding, in conjunction with the Ford Foundation and the Carnegie Corporation, for a children's television program that premiered on public television stations in 1969 and eventually became known as *Sesame Street*. . . .

Legal Services

The Economic Opportunity Act didn't expressly provide for the creation of a legal services program component, but OEO saw the need for legal services for the poor as part of a comprehensive anti-poverty strategy. In 1966, there were 130 legal services programs getting OEO funding; by 1968 the number had doubled to 260 programs. The program designers also recognized the need for a network of supporting programs backing up local legal service agencies, such as a national information clearinghouse as well as legal services programs focused on topics such as housing and employment. Presciently, OEO's legal services effort was based on a now-common understanding of how to strengthen nonprofits by linking them together with sources of technical and financial expertise in distributed networks.

Legal services programs were removed from OEO in 1974 and transferred to an independent Legal Services Corporation, which today provides funding to 136 nonprofit legal services programs around the country, a crucial component of today's nonprofit infrastructure serving the poor.

Job Corps

The problems of youth unemployment are longstanding, but they have been worse during the current recession [2007–2010] than at any time since perhaps the Great Depression. The numbers tell the story: According to the Bureau of Labor Statistics, the labor-force participation rate for all young people age 16 to 24, that is, all young people working or looking for work, fell to 59.5 percent in July [2011], the lowest July rate ever. Only 48.8 percent of the 16-to-24-year-old civilian noninstitutional population is employed, the lowest rate on record. The youth unemployment rate in July was 18.1 percent—20.1 percent for young Hispanics and 31.0 percent for young African-Americans.

How much worse would these numbers be were it not for the existence of the Job Corps, one of the EOA components most strongly supported by President Johnson? The model for the Job Corps was the New Deal's Civilian Conservation Corps, which provided room, board, job training, and employment to thousands of unemployed young people. Since its creation in 1965, there have been close to three million young people who have lived, trained, and worked at Job Corps sites. There are currently about 125 Job Corps sites around the country providing training and vocational employment to about 60,000 young people per year.

Community Action Program

The animus of so many people toward the anti-poverty agenda of the 1960s had little to do with its $1 billion budget or the particular program initiatives that it funded. It was politics. Empowerment of lower-income people, frequently African American or Latino, usually led to a power struggle between the minority leadership of anti-poverty agencies and the typically white power structure of local governments that felt threatened by competing sources of influence and control. At the nexus

of these battles one could often find a federally-funded Community Action agency.

At one time, there were some 1,600 Community Action agencies around the country. About 1,100 still exist, operating a variety of programs, many funded by the remnants of EOA's core program funding, since renamed the Community Services Block Grant (CSBG). . . .

After playing crucial roles in the implementation of core parts of the federal stimulus—particularly the weatherization component, consistently one of the best job creators in the entire stimulus package—

> CHCs [Community Health Centers], . . . community action agencies, legal services corporations, and Head Start agencies . . . are hardly dinosaurs.

Community Action agencies should realize that they have to see themselves not simply as a product of the War on Poverty, but a crucial piece of the nonprofit infrastructure. . . .

Community Health Centers (CHCs)

Neighborhood health clinics for the poor were also a creation of the Economic Opportunity Act. The first ones were demonstration projects in Boston (the Columbia Point Health Center, located in a public housing project) and Mound Bayou, Mississippi (the Delta Health Center). By the early 1970s, they were moved from OEO to the Department of Health, Education and Welfare (HEW, now renamed Health and Human Services). There are now more than 1,100 CHCs, and like community action agencies, legal services corporations, and Head Start agencies, they are hardly dinosaurs. In fact, the number of community health centers today is almost 50 percent larger than it was in 2003. Program funding for community health centers falls under Section 330 of the Public Health Service Act (which is why many federally qualified health centers are called "330 grantees") and gives

Photo on previous page: Three men discuss auto repair complaints in front of a Denver, Colorado, Legal Aid Society office—one of the many social service agencies that grew out of the Great Society's Equal Opportunity Act. (© Duane Howell/ The Denver Post via Getty Images.)

this swath of nonprofit organizational descendants of the Economic Opportunity Act significant responsibilities as health care reform [the Patient Protection and Affordable Care Act of 2010] begins to take hold. . . .

Services and Advocacy Are Equally Important

When it comes to the services needed by the poor, the array of nonprofits with origins in the Economic Opportunity Act of 1964 is the first port of call. In an era when our national leaders are unable to even utter the words "poverty" or "the poor," this infrastructure of nonprofit organizations and nonprofit leaders keeps America's feet to the fire—supporting people and communities most in need, particularly those who don't quite fit the apolitical "middle class" moniker. Moreover, these anti-poverty nonprofits work in partnership with other nonprofits in their communities, adding an element of social and economic equity to the human services work of other groups. And unlike the increasingly bland, narrow conception of nonprofits as just human-service providers, these nonprofits tie advocacy and organizing into their service delivery programs.

> Opponents of empowering the poor are armed with cleavers aimed at social programs under the guise of balancing the federal budget.

That may be why legal services groups and community action agencies earn so much opprobrium from the economic and political forces they confront—and why that combination of functions is so essential to maintain.

Howard Phillips, Donald Rumsfeld, Dick Cheney, Richard Nixon, Ronald Reagan, and others have tried mightily to dismantle the EOA's creation of a nonprofit sector dedicated to fighting poverty. They moved OEO programs to other agencies, combined and separated funding streams, and at times watched idly as the War in Indochina starved the War on Poverty in the U.S. of needed resources. But fighting with and for the poor is always a risky business, never more so than now when rolling budget cuts are threatening the survival of whole swaths of nonprofit capacity.

President [Barack] Obama's willingness to sacrifice the Community Services Block Grant program [by cutting its 2012 budget], regardless of its impact on community action agencies, is simply one indication of a sometimes bipartisan openness to removing essential bricks from the nonprofit anti-poverty edifice. Money designated in the Affordable Care Act for expansion of community health centers has already been cut and more cuts are on the way in the context of budget reform. These federal cuts have been more than matched by state agencies deciding that they cannot or will not fund community health centers the way they did before. Earlier this year [2011], the Republican-dominated House slashed $2 billion from President Obama's $8.2 billion Head Start funding request.

Today, there may not be a single person given the charge of pulling down the nation's nonprofit anti-poverty infrastructure, like Howard Phillips during the Nixon Administration (he actually resigned in frustration when he failed to undo the Great Society's anti-poverty apparatus). However, there are multiple points of pressure on these federally funded nonprofits. The political opponents of empowering the poor are armed with cleavers aimed at social programs under the guise of balancing the federal budget and controlling the federal debt.

The challenge is for the Baby Boomers still in the nonprofit sector and the Gen X'ers now assuming leadership positions to fight to maintain and strengthen the anti-poverty wing of the nonprofit infrastructure. The 47-year-old Economic Opportunity Act may have been born on the cusp of two generations, but it represents the part of the nonprofit sector that fights for social justice for all generations.

Great Society Programs Transformed the Demographics of Higher Education

Thomas Brock

In the following viewpoint, an education researcher reviews the changes in the demographics of higher education in the United States since the reforms of the Great Society. He writes that college students used to be primarily white, male, and from higher-income families. Changes precipitated by legislation such as the Civil Rights Act and Higher Education Act, together with the social activism of the late 1960s, improved the makeup of student populations. Not only did student population grow overall, the author explains, the gender balance reversed, enrollment by all minorities increased, and the proportion of white students decreased. However, two-year colleges have gained a more prominent role, and nonselective institutions enroll the largest proportion of female, black, and Hispanic students. Despite the progress that has been made in diversifying the college population, the author writes, helping students to complete college remains a policy challenge. Thomas Brock is commissioner of the National Center for Education Research, an institute within the US Department of Education. Brock is also the author of numerous journal articles and publications on postsecondary education.

Before 1965, American colleges and universities were rarefied places populated mostly by white males from middle- or upper-income families. In part, the lack of diversity reflected the fact that for much of the nation's history, a college education was not needed to make a decent living. Indeed, after World War II, the difference between the average wages of high school and college graduates was small and shrinking. After 1950, however, the trend moved in the opposite direction and accelerated as the demand for highly skilled labor increased. In 1975, year-round workers with a bachelor's degree earned 1.5 times the annual pay of workers with only a high school diploma; by 1999, that ratio had risen to 1.8.

> "The civil rights movement influenced higher education by challenging public laws and practices that excluded blacks and other minority groups.

Prevailing social norms and a limited federal role in higher education also served to keep higher education an exclusive domain before the 1960s. In many parts of the country, discriminatory laws and attitudes kept many blacks and other racial or ethnic minorities from pursuing a college degree. Prevailing attitudes about the role of women limited their college-going as well. Finally, before 1965, financial aid was not generally available for college students. The federal G.I. Bill [of 1944] had covered college costs for tens of thousands of veterans after World War II, but it, too, had "masculinized" campus life and had aided whites far more than African Americans.

The Transformations of the 1960s

The mid-to-late 1960s marked a major turning point. Changes in federal policy, coupled with big changes in public attitudes and expectations, opened up higher education as never before. From a policy perspective, the passage of the Higher Education Act of 1965 was arguably the most important change, as it extended need-based financial assistance to the general population for the first time. The federal role expanded in other ways, too, fueling growth on college and university campuses. Starting in 1963, for example, the federal government launched a major program for facilities construction, targeting "developing institutions" like community colleges and historically black colleges and universities. Federal spending on higher education increased exponentially, from $655 million in 1956 to $3.5 billion in 1966.

During the same period, the civil rights movement influenced higher education by challenging public laws and practices that excluded blacks and other minority groups from attending some colleges and universities, particularly in the South. Early battles focused on winning admittance for individual students. In 1964, Congress passed the Civil Rights Act, which outlawed discrimination based on race in schools, public places, and employment and mandated equal opportunity for women. By the late 1960s, civil rights activists broadened their perspective to encompass poverty and income inequality and helped launch dozens of Great Society programs that funded education and job training programs targeted to low-income Americans.

Demographic trends, combined with the social activism of the 1960s, also created pressure for change. As the baby boom generation reached maturity, young adults poured onto college campuses in record numbers. Colleges and universities became centers of pro-test, most famously against the Vietnam War, but also against all manner of social convention and custom. Rules governing higher education were not above the fray. Questions of who should have access—and what role colleges and universities should play in confront-ing and reducing inequities in the larger society—were hotly debated. The "open admissions" movement gained currency during this era, most famously with the 1970 decision by the City University of New York to allow all high school graduates to pursue college degrees regardless of academic preparation. Other institutions across the country, notably community colleges, adopted similar policies.

> Along with increased enroll-ments, the demographics of students attending colleges and universities changed.

Changes in Student Enrollment and Demographics

The effects of changing laws and attitudes are evident in the dramatic rise in college enrollments. . . . Total fall enrollment increased from just over 5.9 million students in 1965 to about 17.5 million students in 2005—a nearly 300 percent increase. The rise was steepest through 1975 and was far greater than could be accounted for by popu-lation growth alone. To put the enrollment figures into perspective, in 1965 the number of young adults in the prime college-going years of eighteen to twenty-four was approximately 20.3 million; by 2005 that number had increased 44 percent, to about 29.2 million.

Along with increased enrollments, the demograph-ics of students attending colleges and universities changed. . . . The gender balance reversed between 1970 and 2005, from mostly male to mostly female. The . . . percentage of students from racial or ethnic minority groups . . . more than doubled from 1976 to 2005. By

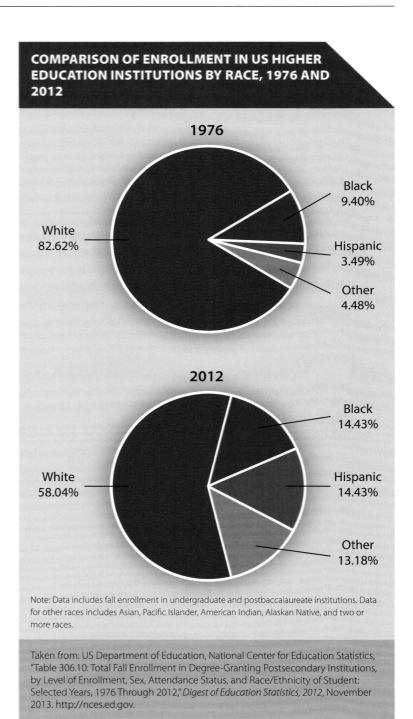

COMPARISON OF ENROLLMENT IN US HIGHER EDUCATION INSTITUTIONS BY RACE, 1976 AND 2012

1976

White
82.62%

Black
9.40%

Hispanic
3.49%

Other
4.48%

2012

White
58.04%

Black
14.43%

Hispanic
14.43%

Other
13.18%

Note: Data includes fall enrollment in undergraduate and postbaccalaureate institutions. Data for other races includes Asian, Pacific Islander, American Indian, Alaskan Native, and two or more races.

Taken from: US Department of Education, National Center for Education Statistics, "Table 306.10: Total Fall Enrollment in Degree-Granting Postsecondary Institutions, by Level of Enrollment, Sex, Attendance Status, and Race/Ethnicity of Student: Selected Years, 1976 Through 2012," *Digest of Education Statistics, 2012*, November 2013. http://nces.ed.gov.

far the largest percentage increases were among Hispanics and Asian and Pacific Islanders, though all minority groups experienced growth in college enrollment while the share of whites declined. . . . The percentage of students aged twenty-five and older [increased with] a proportionate decline in those aged twenty-four and under. The U.S. Department of Education projects that the trend toward older students will continue in coming years.

The shift in demographic characteristics hints at another significant development in the student population. The so-called traditional undergraduate—the high school graduate who enrolls full-time immediately after finishing high school, relies on parents for financial support, and either does not work during the school year or works only part-time—is now the exception rather than the rule. Only 27 percent of undergraduates met these criteria in 1999–2000. By comparison, in the same year, 28 percent of undergraduates met the Department of Education's definition of "highly nontraditional": they were likely in their twenties or older, working while going to school, and raising children (possibly as single parents), among other criteria. Some highly nontraditional students did not have a high school diploma.

> " The demographic composition of colleges and universities has become more diverse over the past forty years. "

Changes in Types of Institutions Attended

Government statistics show that a large majority of undergraduates enroll in four-year colleges and universities. At the same time, the "center of gravity" in higher education has gradually shifted, with community colleges playing a much more prominent role today than in the past. In 1969 (when the government adopted its current methodology for categorizing two- and four-year schools), 26 percent of all college students attended two-year institutions. By 2005, that figure had risen to 37 percent.

The vast majority of students enroll in publicly funded colleges and universities. In 2005, private institutions accounted for about one-fourth of all undergraduates—a figure that has increased only slightly in the past decade. Nearly all of these students are enrolled in four-year institutions, though a small percentage of students is enrolled in private two-year colleges. The advent of on-line courses may be changing higher education again. Indeed, two of the five largest higher education institutions in 2005 rely principally on online instruction: the University of Phoenix, with an enrollment of more than 117,000 students, and Western International University, with an enrollment of nearly 51,000 students.

Although the demographic composition of colleges and universities has become more diverse over the past forty years, the increased diversity is largely accounted for by nonselective institutions. Specifically, female, black, and Hispanic students are disproportionately enrolled in community colleges. Nontraditional students are also much more likely to be enrolled in community colleges and to participate in distance education via the Internet.

Trends in Student Persistence and Completion

Government statistics indicate that student outcomes differ markedly by type of institution attended. Specifically, undergraduates who begin at four-year colleges and universities are about twice as likely to complete a postsecondary degree as undergraduates who begin at two-year institutions. The five-year completion rate for students who began at a four-year college or university—taking into account certificates, associate's degrees, or bachelor's degrees—was 60 percent in the 1995–96 academic year. For students who began at a community college, the rate of completion was 32 percent.

Many students take longer than five years to earn a degree: some are enrolled part-time, some change their majors, some need to drop out temporarily, and some have other reasons for the delay. Measures of *persistence* take into account those who have earned a certificate or degree as well as those who are still enrolled in college. Eighty percent of students who began at a four-year college or university in 1995–96 persisted after five years. Among students who began at a community college, the persistence rate was 52 percent. The data also show that students attending private institutions (both four-year and two-year) persist at higher rates than their counterparts at public institutions.

Viewed historically, rates of completion at four-year institutions have been unchanged since the federal government began collecting data during the 1970s. A recent study suggests that there has been a slight uptick in the persistence rate at public four-year colleges. Although that increase may seem contradictory, it likely reflects the longer time it now takes students in four-year colleges, particularly at less selective public institutions, to earn degrees. Historical data on students attending community college go back only to 1990, but show no significant change in persistence or completion.

Persistence and completion rates differ significantly by race and ethnicity and by gender. At public two- and four-year institutions, Asian and Pacific Islanders have the highest persistence and completion rates of any racial or ethnic group, followed by non-Hispanic whites, Hispanics, and non-Hispanic blacks. (The longitudinal studies commissioned by the government lack sufficient numbers of American Indians and Alaska Natives on which to report.) Asian and Pacific Islanders who entered public four-year institutions in 1995–96 were

Vivian Malone, the first African American graduate of the University of Alabama, walks past the registration desks at the school in June 1963. (© Rolls Press/ **Popperfoto/Getty Images.**)

nearly twice as likely to earn a degree or still be in school after six years as non-Hispanic blacks who entered the same year. The story by gender is a bit more complicated. At public four-year institutions, women have slightly higher persistence and completion rates than men (a difference of about 5 percentage points); at public two-year institutions, the gender difference is reversed. It is important to recall that because more women than men enroll in college, many more associate's and bachelor's degrees are awarded to women—a pattern that has held true at both two- and four-year institutions since at least the late 1980s.

Despite these patterns, neither race and ethnicity nor gender is a good predictor of who will earn a college degree, owing to large variation within these demographic groups. Research by Clifford Adelman for the Department of Education shows that the two best predictors are entering college immediately after finishing high school and taking a high school curriculum that stresses reading at grade level and math beyond basic algebra. Higher socioeconomic status is also a predictor, though only moderately so. Consistent with these findings, being classified as a traditional student is another strong predictor of college completion. Conversely, all of the characteristics used to define nontraditional status—delayed entry into college from high school, working full-time, single parenthood, and so on—are considered "risk factors" because they are negatively correlated with persistence. As noted, community colleges account for a disproportionate share of nontraditional students; they are also the institutions that raise the most concern about persistence and completion.

> College access remains problematic, and gaps in enrollment between certain racial and ethnic minority groups are substantial.

More Students but Little Progress

Access to higher education has been greatly expanded since the mid-1960s. More students are attending college—both in real terms and as a percentage of the population—and they are demographically more diverse. Actions taken by the federal government clearly played a major part in these trends, though larger economic, demographic, and social forces were also at play. Finally, the growth of nonselective institutions like community colleges and, more recently, online courses and programs has made it easier for people to attend college even if they lack good preparation or are working while going to school.

Despite these gains, college access remains problematic, and gaps in enrollment between certain racial and ethnic minority groups are substantial. In 2006, for example, 44 percent of whites between the ages of eighteen and twenty-four were enrolled in college, compared with 32 percent of blacks and 25 percent of Hispanics. Rates of college attendance for black and Hispanic males are particularly low. A recent national survey of college-qualified students who did not enroll in college underscores that college costs, availability of aid, and uncertainty about the steps needed to enroll in college remain significant deterrents. Inadequate preparation for college is another factor, though with the rise of nonselective institutions, it is less a barrier to access than to success once students have enrolled in college.

From a public policy standpoint, it makes little sense to promote greater college access if students are failing once they get there. Figuring out how to boost college completion is the challenge. The United States has seen no progress on this measure since the advent of statistics on it and is losing ground to other nations in the share of the adult population with college degrees. The costs of such failure—to students especially, but also to colleges, governments, and society at large—are extremely high.

Despite Partisan Attacks, Americans Value the Cultural Endowments Established by the Great Society

Cynthia Koch

In the following viewpoint, a historian and policy researcher discusses the history of the National Endowment for the Arts (NEA) and National Endowment for the Humanities (NEH). Both organizations were started by Great Society legislation signed into law by Lyndon B. Johnson in 1965. However, the author writes, the organizations have their roots in the Works Progress Administration programs of the 1930s, New Deal and cultural programs created during World War II. The author explains that

SOURCE. Cynthia Koch, "The Contest for American Culture: A Leadership Case Study on the NEA and NEH Funding Crisis," *Public Talk*, 1998, pp. 5–8, 21–22, 23–24, 26–27. Copyright © 1998 by Trustees of the University of Pennsylvania. All rights reserved. Reproduced by permission.

while popular support for federal cultural funding grew during the 1960s, there was an ideological split between the politicians who supported such funding and those who did not. When the endowments were created, however, they enjoyed the support of a bipartisan group of leaders. That dynamic changed with the Ronald Reagan administration starting in 1981. The author explains that, at the turn of the twenty-first century, there was debate about the value of the endowments to American society, but the endowments have shown that there is a legitimate role for federal government support of culture. Cynthia Koch is the former director of the Franklin D. Roosevelt Presidential Library and Museum.

The National Foundation for the Arts and Humanities Act of 1965 provided for the establishment of a National Council on the Arts and a National Council for the Humanities, the two endowments [the National Endowment for the Arts (NEA) and the National Endowment for the Humanities (NEH)], and ultimately arts and humanities councils in every state. The two endowments probably trace their roots most directly to the Depression-era WPA [Works Progress Administration] programs: the Federal Art Project, Federal Music Project, Federal Writers Project, and Federal Theater Project. Besides providing needed employment for artists, they also gave many Americans their first experience with "public art" as communities dealt with artists on civic boards determining standards for highly visible public commissions in schools, post offices, and city halls. Art and artists were no longer the province of the "high" society of art museums and symphony orchestras, but rather of society as a whole.

During the Depression some legislation was proposed at the federal level that would have had the power to institutionalize some of these activities on a permanent basis. But with the beginning of World War II, the political will to establish a national cultural agency disappeared. As the economy improved, WPA legislation was phased out and conditions largely returned to their pre-war stasis: government support for the art—with the exception of practical necessities such as monuments and military bands—was perceived as a frill and outside the legitimate realm of government support. During the war the government sponsored propagandistic arts projects to advance the war effort; but with the exception of programs sponsored by the Office of Inter-American Affairs [OIAA] (headed by Nelson Rockefeller), which sponsored tours and cultural exchanges with Latin America, whatever modest arts funding existed was usually buried in the budgets of non-arts programs.

> "Arts and humanities advocates were generally liberal. . . . Their opponents were often from the South or rural areas and frequently anti-intellectual."

The immediate precursor of the national endowments came as an extension of Rockefeller's activities with the OIAA during World War II. In 1954 Rockefeller, then an undersecretary in [Dwight D.] Eisenhower's Department of Health, Education, and Welfare, developed a plan based on the Arts Council of Great Britain to create a National Council on the Arts. But necessary legislation failed in Congress. Nancy Hanks, who worked for Rockefeller at the time and was later to become a popular chair of the NEA, described the derision with which this proposal was met in Congress where the bill was referred to as the "President's toe dance bill." Nonetheless, according to Hanks, this legislation saw life a few years later in 1960 when Rockefeller became governor of New York and it served as the model for the New York State Council on the Arts.

The 1965 federal legislation was also patterned after the 1954 bill (according to Hanks) and it was in that year that cultural and educational advocacy efforts in a number of areas finally coalesced. The Rockefeller Panel

Report, *The Performing Arts: Problems and Prospects*, made front page news describing serious funding problems in some the nation's largest arts organizations. The Elementary and Secondary School Act, authorizing schools to "develop innovative projects which . . . utilize the service of arts groups and cultural resources in their communities" was passed, and a crucial piece of legislation was crafted in Congress that brought together the parallel but divergent efforts of arts and humanities advocates. . . .

The Conservative/Liberal Divide

As support for cultural funding grew, longstanding political divisions that had stymied previous federal efforts became more public as debate intensified. Arts and humanities advocates were generally liberal Democrats and Republicans, while conservatives of both parties espoused small government and untrammeled free enterprise. Not insignificantly, arts and humanities supporters were also well educated and drawn from urban areas where many leading cultural and educational institutions were and still are concentrated. Their opponents were often from the South or rural areas and frequently anti-intellectual.

By 1965, the year of the successful legislation that combined the two separate arts and humanities advocacy efforts into a single National Foundation on the Arts and Humanities Act, more than 100 separate bills in favor of cultural funding were introduced in the 89th Congress. . . .

Opponents in the early 1960s used arguments against the endowments that still ring familiar: "With the nation $290 billion in debt," declared Rep. Howard Gross of Iowa, "an additional $200,000 each year for a council might be better deferred until we have a balanced budget in this country and start retiring the Federal debt." Rep. Howard Smith of Virginia, an outspoken foe and chair-

The 1989 NEA Serrano-Mapplethorpe Controversy

The . . . uproar over National Endowment for the Arts [NEA] funding of controversial artists began in [April] 1989, when the Rev. Donald Wildmon of the conservative American Family Association of Tupelo, Missouri, held a press conference to denounce NEA funding of "anti-Christian bigotry," referring to the exhibition of Andres Serrano's work, which included a photograph, *Piss Christ*, of a crucifix submerged in the artist's urine. The controversy later expanded to include the work of other artists, including Robert Mapplethorpe, Annie Sprinkle, and others. Shortly after the American Family Association's press conference, Senators Jesse Helms (R-NC) and Alfonse D'Amato (R-NY) denounced Serrano's work; thirty-six senators signed a "letter to the NEA expressing outrage." Rep. Dick Armey, a Republican from Texas and long-time opponent of federal arts support, [sent] a letter signed by 107 representatives to the NEA [calling] attention to a retrospective entitled *Robert Mapplethorpe: The Perfect Moment*, scheduled to open at Washington [DC]'s Corcoran Gallery of Art in July [1989]. He [labeled] the works of both artists as "morally reprehensible trash."

SOURCE. Margaret Quigley, "The Mapplethorpe Censorship Controversy: Chronology of Events," *Political Research Associates*. www.publiceye.org /theocrat/Mapplethorpe_Chrono.html.

man of the powerful House Rules Committee, displayed his animosity for the cultural elite:

> What are the arts? And here is where I display my ignorance. I do not know. . . . I suppose fiddle players would be in the arts and the painting of pictures would be in the arts. It was suggested that poker playing would be an artful occupation. Is this going to subsidize poker players that get in trouble?

In Senate debate over the National Arts and Cultural Development Act in 1963, another precursor to the final legislation, [South Carolina senator] Strom Thurmond was the only opponent of the bill to speak. Doubting the constitutionality of arts subsidies, he objected to the supporters' contention that government involvement in arts subsidies was covered under the "general welfare" clause and raised the specter of government control of the arts: "the Federal Government has the power to control that which it subsidizes and experience proves that when the Federal Government has the power, that power is eventually exercised." This argument of the defeated opposition would surface again and again in the next thirty years. . . .

Early Bipartisan Support

At the time of their founding the endowments were championed by a powerful group of bipartisan leaders: Presidents [John F.] Kennedy and [Lyndon] Johnson, Nelson Rockefeller, and a group of influential senators and congressmen. [US president] Richard Nixon, never a friend of the endowments, nevertheless found political advantage in their support. At the urging of Leonard Garment, his "arts loving saxophone playing legal aide," he oversaw substantial increases in the endowments budgets at least until his 1972 nomination was secure. Also under Nixon (although credit for them must go to [Rhode Island senator] Claiborne Pell), the state humanities councils were organized, expanding public programs in the humanities to local communities through relatively modest grants to the states and, not incidentally, building a political base for the humanities in local communities. Budget growth continued during the [Jimmy] Carter Administration accompanied by a number of initiatives at both endowments that extended the reach of the arts and humani-

> Critics [in the 1980s] made their arguments on political grounds that opposed the expansion of arts and humanities programs.

ties to minority communities and other nontraditional audiences.

With the election of Ronald Reagan [in 1980], however, the dynamic shifted. Critics at the time made their arguments on political grounds that opposed the expansion of arts and humanities programs to traditionally Democratic constituencies. The Heritage Foundation report prepared at the time of Reagan's election decried the NEA's Expansion Arts Program (described in the endowment's 1979 annual report as "a point of entry for developing groups that are established in and reflect the culture of minority, blue collar, rural and low-income communities") as an example of the dilution of aesthetic standards. The NEH was lambasted for sacrificing "scholarly excellence" in favor of "political" projects that did not properly belong "in the realm of humanities." A 1980 grant of $199,953 to a group called the Working Women: National Association of Office Workers, which held classes and film forums on the struggle of office workers for improved conditions, was criticized as an example of the politicization of the humanities with "populist" or "social action" programs considered to have little scholarly merit. . . .

However, it was not until the Mapplethorpe-Serrano controversy, when the religious Right joined the political Right, that criticism of the NEA captured national attention. . . .

The Role of the Media

The number of articles on either the NEA or NEH appearing in major newspapers for the twenty-year period since the late 1970s, [show] the rise and fall of their public visibility coinciding with the major assaults on the agencies by conservative activists. Most articles in the late 1970s and 1980s were carried in the *Washington Post* or the *New York Times;* modest increases in coverage are registered for 1981 and again [in] 1985,

An artwork by Andres Serrano titled *Immersion Piss Christ* was at the center of a 1989 controversy about funding for the National Endowment for the Arts. (Damage shown in this 2011 photo was caused by Roman Catholic activists who believed the artwork to be profane.) (© **Boris Horvat/ AFP/Getty Images.**)

when early budget cutting efforts were initiated. But in 1989–90 with Mapplethorpe-Serrano, the number of articles skyrocketed and expanded to include newspapers across the country. The *Boston Globe, Los Angeles Times, USA Today, St. Petersburg Times, Newsday, San Francisco Chronicle, Orange County Register, St. Louis Post Dispatch, Chicago Tribune, San Diego Union-Tribune, Courier-Journal* (Louisville, KY), and *Christian Science Monitor* regularly covered the controversy. In the early 1990s the number of articles moderated slightly but never again dipped to the nearly invisible levels that the endowments had earlier enjoyed. Coverage by newspapers throughout the country became regular; no longer was the fate of the endowments presumed to be of interest only to the readers of the *Washington Post* and the *New York Times*. The content of the coverage also changed. Earlier debates over budget growth, quality, and politicization of the endowments were replaced by appeals to emotion in the charges of pornography and attacks on the cultural elite. A June 1989 *Washington Times* editorial by Patrick Buchanan, founder of the Christian Coalition, was a clarion call for what would become the culture wars of the 1990s:

> The decade has seen an explosion of anti-American, anti-Christian, and nihilist "art." . . . [Many museums] now feature exhibits that can best be described as cultural trash . . . as in public television and public radio, a tiny clique, out of touch with America's traditional values, has wormed its way into control of the arts bureaucracy. . . . As with our rivers and lakes, we need to clean up our culture: for it is a well from which we must all drink. Just as a poisoned land will yield up poisonous fruits, so a polluted culture, left to fester and stink, can destroy a nation's soul. . . . We should not subsidize decadence.

Participants were forced to take sides in an all-or-nothing, winner-take-all conflict that was largely fought in the media. Citizen outrage expressed to members of Congress was the ammunition and budget cuts to the cultural endowments were the spoils of war. The mediated nature of virtually all communication on the issues put rational argument at a disadvantage. Simplification and emotionalism on the part of the opponents were more powerful and

> "As press coverage increased, the endowments' budgets declined over the past twenty years."

effective than the defenders' appeals to free speech and "good news" stories about the agencies' many successes. . . . Public criticism of the endowments has always been an effective tool for opponents: as press coverage increased, the endowments' budgets declined over the past twenty years. Nervous members of Congress counted the postcards, telephone calls, and letters from constituents as harbingers of public sentiment, but in the end news coverage meant criticism, which translated into fewer cultural dollars. . . .

The Continuing Cultural Wars

The years between the founding of the endowments and the conservative assault saw dramatic shifts in the position of the arts and humanities in America. Born out of a Cold War and Great Society ethos that trumpeted American achievement in the arts and scholarship as a point of national pride, by the 1990s critics charged artists and scholars with being destructive of the American family and un-American; the endowments, as their federally funded standard bearers, had to be abolished for the good of the country. Cultural advocates, forced to defend themselves, truly became politicized; they turned to their allies in communities and institutions and marshaled public and Congressional support for their survival. Deeply affected by the debate, cultural advocates are wary now. They have learned to live with lower budgets and in the public eye, self-censoring and careful to avoid public controversy. But many also learned the importance of funding and delivering programs that have meaning and value for Americans in all their geographic and demographic diversity.

> There is a bipartisan consensus . . . for a legitimate role for the federal government in the support of American culture.

Is the conflict over? Probably not. Doctrinaire conservative opinion makers continue to oppose the endowments as evidenced on the websites of the Cato Institute, Heritage Foundation, and Family Research Council—all of which continue to carry position statements advocating the abolition of the endowments in the summer of 1998. . . . For the most part, opposition to the NEH seems to have once again receded to the background, while opposition to the NEA on "family values" grounds continues—as it has since the Mapplethorpe-Serrano controversy—to animate opposition from the religious Right.

But there are encouraging signs in the middle, which may well represent the enduring victory of the culture wars. A rancorous and emotional public debate that was started by radical conservatives with the goal of damaging the cultural endowments may ultimately prove to have strengthened them. Because, in the contest for the endowments' survival, members of Congress heard from citizens across the country about support for the arts and humanities and learned that culture is no longer the province of the few. The president listened, and whether from political instinct or personal preference, appointed endowments chairmen whose scholarly and artistic specialties reflect the broad interests of Americans whose culture has long been considered outside the province of high art and serious scholarship.

No longer championed unquestioningly by presidents and powerful friends in Congress, the endowments in the [1990s] have been the subject of a national debate centered around their value in American society. The debate has been messy, as politics always are, but the result has been a demonstration that culture in America has many faces. It has strong roots in local communities and in a variety of artistic and intellectual traditions. The Christian conservatives may never be satisfied; but in the contest for control of American culture, the endowments, albeit battle scarred and perhaps chastened, can take heart in the knowledge that their right to exist has been proved in Congress and in the court of public opinion.

Legitimizing a Federal Role in Culture

What that signifies is enormous. It means that the most extreme charges have been put aside and that there is a bipartisan consensus—very likely for the first time since the endowments' founding—for a legitimate role for the federal government in the support of American culture. Charges of elitism and domination by East Coast intellectuals and moneyed interests simply did not hold up under public scrutiny when arts and humanities organizations from across the country demonstrated that local communities in Kansas and Utah, Washington, and Mississippi value the federal agencies.

It also means that the new leadership of the endowments have an unparalleled opportunity. For the past decade millions of Americans have engaged in a national conversation in defense of the arts and humanities. Now is the time to keep that conversation going by involving an even greater number of Americans from all walks of life in exploring the world of ideas. If this is accomplished, the NEA and the NEH can look forward to playing an even more important role in our national life in the decades to come.

Head Start Was Based on the Belief That Early Education Can Eradicate Poverty

Barbara T. Bowman

In the following viewpoint, an early education expert discusses the history of Head Start and the values that drove its development. She explains that Head Start's mission of improving low-income children's development was the product of support from developmental research, governmental activism, and the civil rights movement. The program was one of the programs engendered by the Great Society's War on Poverty and was administered directly by the Office of Economic Opportunity, the author writes. The program employed different models to provide comprehensive services for children, including medical or dental care, summer programs, and training for parents. Research to track Head Start's successes and failures was incorporated early on in the process. As a result, its components, monitoring, and standards are the benchmarks in the field of childhood education, she writes. According to the author, Head Start has not only contributed to the education of poor children but to the understanding of child development and learning, and it should continue its tradition of adaptation and improvement. Barbara T. Bowman is one of the founders of the Erikson Institute, a graduate school in child development. She was previously chief early childhood education officer for the Chicago Public Schools and a former consultant to Secretary of Education Arne Duncan.

In the 21st century, how we care for and educate young children is gaining public attention as Americans recognize that the out-of-home care and education delivery systems are not serving children and families as well as they should or could. Many children are not receiving the quality of services they need to develop optimally and succeed in school. To remedy this will require careful and systemic planning that takes into account past, current, and future social and economic constraints and opportunities. Inevitably, Head Start, our largest and most important national program for children, has a critical role to play. As we are now in a new millennium, it is a good time to review the contribution Head Start has made and consider how it can be adapted to the challenges of tomorrow.

Head Start's Origins

The original mission of Head Start was to foster the development of children from low-income families. A history of limited health, social service, education, and employment opportunities compromised the development of many such children, and they were ill prepared for school. Head Start was to provide the human and material capital necessary to assure their healthy development and school readiness.

Support for the Head Start mission came from three directions: developmental research, governmental activism, and the civil rights movement. Research provided evidence that children's intelligence is malleable, the environment is critical in shaping it, and early childhood is an important period for development. This research suggested that young children from low-income families needed a range of social, psychological, health and nutrition, and educational services to enhance their development and, consequently, their school achievement. Pilot programs demonstrated the feasibility of this approach.

> Head Start was born as one of a number of programs making up the War on Poverty.

Governmental activism, spurred during the depression and war years, resulted in a number of 20th-century initiatives to redress social problems. During the first half of the 20th century, health, labor, welfare, and education legislation was passed to promote children's well-being. For example, public schools required vaccinations for school attendance, child labor laws limited the number of hours children could work, financial assistance was made available to families with dependent children, and Work Projects Administration and Lanham Act nurseries provided care and education during national emergencies.

The civil rights movement, led by African Americans after the Second World War, agitated for the end to racial segregation. The greater economic and social security of middle-class and white Americans undoubtedly contributed to the public willingness for government to address social inequities and the needs of children. Finally, in the 1960s, there was sufficient political will to pass the civil rights and economic opportunity bills, which energized national efforts on behalf of low-income and minority groups.

Against this backdrop, Head Start was born as one of a number of programs making up the War on Poverty. The Office of Economic Opportunity (OEO) administered the program directly from Washington, D.C., and under its aegis, low-income people were encouraged to make decisions about how funds were to be used, thus combining political, economic, and social service objectives. Because OEO was a federal agency, it was able to make a commitment to social justice and community empowerment, even though these goals were not favored in some of the states and localities where programs were opened.

Social Values and Head Start's Mission

Head Start was infused with these goals. It reflected the understanding that children's development is tied to their families and communities. To effect change, parents and community members needed to be educated and supported, so Head Start encouraged, indeed required, parents to make their own decisions about Head Start goals and objectives, curricula, staff, and budgets. There was no single model of Head Start. At various times and places, its purposes included empowering parents, employing community members, registering voters, redressing caste and class discrimination, arranging health care, providing social services, supporting children's cognitive development, and/or teaching children academic skills.

Despite its community action orientation, Head Start's central mission was to provide comprehensive services for children. The expectation was that Head Start interventions could be accomplished quickly and would have great benefits for children. For example, in communities where health services were not available through public or private means, Head Start contracted and paid for medical and dental care. Head Start's educational program was to be brief—summer-long, then year-long. At that time, few American children were enrolled in preschool, and in some states, even public kindergarten was not available. Therefore, the short educational program would confer an advantage on low-income children, giving them a head start on school. Parents, by volunteering in the center and attending parent meetings, would learn new child-rearing practices, which would enhance children's development.

Staff training was an early focus of Head Start. In the late 1960s, there were few well-trained professionals skilled in working with low-income families and preschool-age children. Not only did the Head Start program include a strong in-service education program, but it also provided college and graduate school tuition for staff interested in formal education. Head Start staffs included teachers, administrators, social workers, nurses,

A part-time aide (left) and a local project coordinator review the day's activities at a Head Start in Commerce City, Colorado, in 1965. (© Bill Johnson/ The Denver Post via Getty Images.)

and psychologists, while physicians and dentists were often retained to provide direct services. Professionals were regularly engaged to monitor, assess, and report on the quality of the programs. It was a time of social activism, and volunteers—parents, professionals, and community members—were encouraged to be involved.

The first summer programs were housed (and largely staffed) by public schools. There was, however, considerable reluctance to formally lodge the new program in schools (the primary agency for children in localities) because politicians and administrators saw local educational bureaucracies as cumbersome and expensive, early childhood specialists considered traditional school practice (formal instruction) inappropriate for young children, and schools were disinclined to take on an age cohort with which they had no experience. Thus, outside of the big cities, public schools were less and less involved as Head Start developed. The majority of programs were located in small, not-for-profit agencies and religious institutions, and articulation between Head Start and public schools became tenuous.

> The first few years of Head Start were a time of almost frenetic activity, excitement, enthusiasm, and hope.

Research Improves Early Education

The first few years of Head Start were a time of almost frenetic activity, excitement, enthusiasm, and hope, with new initiatives going off in almost every conceivable direction. Within a few years, however, controversies arose. Was Head Start effective? In what way? What were the desirable components? How should they be organized? How should Head Start balance its mission and means between community action and early childhood education?

A robust research agenda was soon undertaken, funded by government and private foundations, which eagerly tracked both Head Start's successes and failures. The broad sweep of Head Start objectives made it a complex organization to administer. Variation was the norm, and administrative control, necessarily loose, unfortunately often led to programs

> "Head Start has been a beacon of hope for many children and families."

with little educational benefit for children. Order was gradually established in programs, largely through the efforts of Edward Zigler and the Office of Child Development (OCD) in the Department of Health, Education and Welfare. Gradually, Head Start became a leader in the field of early childhood education, and Head Start components, monitoring, and performance standards defined the leading edge for good early childhood practice. . . .

Looking to the Future

Over the years, Head Start has been a beacon of hope for many children and families. As a long-term admirer of the contribution of Head Start parents, teachers, and administrators, I share with others a reluctance to change it. Head Start has contributed not only to the education of low-income children, but, through research and demonstration programs, it has also made a lasting contribution to our understanding of children's development and learning. Few in our field will forget Head Start's emphasis on the whole child and comprehensive services. Nevertheless, as we go forward it is important to continue Head Start's tradition of adaptation and improvement. Much can be gained if Head Start continues to analyze the changes in society and considers policy and program alternatives. Head Start has served well in the past. I am certain that the Head Start heritage will live on no matter what its future directions.

Fifty Years Later, Progress on Building a Great Society Continues

Barack Obama

The following viewpoint comes from a 2014 speech by the president of the United States commemorating the fiftieth anniversary of the Civil Rights Act. He says that President Lyndon B. Johnson (LBJ) believed in fighting for his convictions, and he thanks the many Americans who worked together during the civil rights movement. He shares LBJ's belief that government has the power to foster social progress. Johnson, he says, was the product of a disadvantaged childhood during which he learned that poverty and injustice are inseparable, and he used his unique capacity as president to dismantle the structures of oppression and provide new opportunities. The promise of the Great Society may not yet be complete, but the President exhorts the country to follow the example of the men and women of the civil rights movement. Barack Obama is the forty-fourth president of the United States.

SOURCE. Barack Obama, "Remarks by the President at LBJ Presidential Library Civil Rights Summit," Lyndon B. Johnson Presidential Library, April 10, 2014.

F our days into his sudden presidency—and the night before he would address a joint session of the Congress in which he once served—Lyndon Johnson [LBJ] sat around a table with his closest advisors, preparing his remarks to a shattered and grieving nation.

He wanted to call on senators and representatives to pass a civil rights bill—the most sweeping since Reconstruction. And most of his staff counseled him against it. They said it was hopeless; that it would anger powerful Southern Democrats and committee chairmen; that it risked derailing the rest of his domestic agenda. And one particularly bold aide said he did not believe a President should spend his time and power on lost causes, however worthy they might be. To which, it is said, President Johnson replied, "Well, what the hell's the presidency for?" What the hell's the presidency for if not to fight for causes you believe in?

Today [April 10, 2014], as we commemorate the 50th anniversary of the Civil Rights Act, we honor the men and women who made it possible. Some of them are here today. We celebrate giants like John Lewis and Andrew Young and Julian Bond. We recall the countless unheralded Americans, black and white, students and scholars, preachers and housekeepers—whose names are etched not on monuments, but in the hearts of their loved ones, and in the fabric of the country they helped to change.

But we also gather here, deep in the heart of the state that shaped him, to recall one giant man's remarkable efforts to make real the promise of our founding: "We hold these truths to be self-evident, that all men are created equal."

The Presidency as an Agent of Change

Those of us who have had the singular privilege to hold the office of the Presidency know well that progress in this country can be hard and it can be slow, frustrating and sometimes you're stymied. The office humbles you.

You're reminded daily that in this great democracy, you are but a relay swimmer in the currents of history, bound by decisions made by those who came before, reliant on the efforts of those who will follow to fully vindicate your vision.

But the presidency also affords a unique opportunity to bend those currents—by shaping our laws and by shaping our debates; by working within the confines of the world as it is, but also by reimagining the world as it should be.

This was President Johnson's genius. As a master of politics and the legislative process, he grasped like few others the power of government to bring about change.

LBJ was nothing if not a realist. He was well aware that the law alone isn't enough to change hearts and minds. A full century after [Abraham] Lincoln's time, he said, "Until justice is blind to color, until education is unaware of race, until opportunity is unconcerned with the color of men's skins, emancipation will be a proclamation but not a fact."

He understood laws couldn't accomplish everything. But he also knew that only the law could anchor change, and set hearts and minds on a different course. And a lot of Americans needed the law's most basic protections at that time. As Dr. King [Martin Luther King Jr.] said at the time, "It may be true that the law can't make a man love me but it can keep him from lynching me, and I think that's pretty important." . . .

> [President Johnson] knew that only the law could anchor change, and set hearts and minds on a different course.

Johnson's Personal Experience of Poverty

As a young boy growing up in the Texas Hill Country, Johnson knew what being poor felt like. "Poverty was so common," he would later say, "we didn't even know it

had a name." The family home didn't have electricity or indoor plumbing. Everybody worked hard, including the children. President Johnson had known the metallic taste of hunger; the feel of a mother's calloused hands, rubbed raw from washing and cleaning and holding a household together. His cousin Ava remembered sweltering days spent on her hands and knees in the cotton fields, with Lyndon whispering beside her, "Boy, there's got to be a better way to make a living than this. There's got to be a better way."

It wasn't until years later when he was teaching at a so-called Mexican school in a tiny town in Texas that he came to understand how much worse the persistent pain of poverty could be for other races in a Jim Crow South. Oftentimes his students would show up to class hungry. And when he'd visit their homes, he'd meet fathers who were paid slave wages by the farmers they worked for.

The director of the LBJ Presidential Library, Mark Updegrove (left), leads President Barack Obama, First Lady Michelle Obama, and US representative and civil rights icon John Lewis on a tour of the facilities. They were at the library to attend the Civil Rights Summit commemorating the fiftieth anniversary of the Civil Rights Act in April 2014. (© AP Photo/ Carolyn Kaster.)

> Poverty and injustice are as inseparable as opportunity and justice are joined.

Those children were taught, he would later say, "that the end of life is in a beet row, a spinach field, or a cotton patch."

Deprivation and discrimination— these were not abstractions to Lyndon Baines Johnson. He knew that poverty and injustice are as inseparable as opportunity and justice are joined. So that was in him from an early age.

Now, like any of us, he was not a perfect man. His experiences in rural Texas may have stretched his moral imagination, but he was ambitious, very ambitious, a young man in a hurry to plot his own escape from poverty and to chart his own political career. And in the Jim Crow South, that meant not challenging convention. During his first 20 years in Congress, he opposed every civil rights bill that came up for a vote, once calling the push for federal legislation "a farce and a sham." He was chosen as a vice presidential nominee in part because of his affinity with, and ability to deliver, that Southern white vote. And at the beginning of the [John F.] Kennedy administration, he shared with President Kennedy a caution towards racial controversy.

Acting to Transform the Country

But marchers kept marching. Four little girls were killed in a church [bombing in Birmingham, Alabama, on September 15, 1963]. Bloody Sunday [an attack on civil rights demonstrators by state troopers outside Selma, Alabama, on March 7, 1965] happened. The winds of change blew. And when the time came, when LBJ stood in the Oval Office—I picture him standing there, taking up the entire doorframe, looking out over the South Lawn in a quiet moment—and asked himself what the true purpose of his office was for, what was the endpoint of his ambitions, he would reach back in his own memory and he'd remember his own experience with want.

Great Society Programs Harmed African Americans

President [Lyndon] Johnson's War on Poverty, which was being formulated during the [John F.] Kennedy Administration, is perhaps the only government institution that destroyed and devastated the black American upward mobility and family structure. As an assistant secretary of labor, Daniel Patrick Moynihan warned that the premise and concept of the War on Poverty would be detrimental to black America. The infamous split between the races that Moynihan predicted has created a deficit between white and black in key areas such as education, income and net worth. Yet we keep doing the same thing repeatedly hoping for a different result.

SOURCE. *Charles Butler, quoted in "LBJ's 'War on Poverty' Hurt Black Americans; Five Decades After: Black Progress Hurt by Expansion in Government, Welfare; Black Activists Criticize Handout Mentality That Destroyed Traditional Families," Project 21/National Center for Public Policy Research, January 8, 2014. www.nationalcenter.org /P21PR-WarOnPoverty_010814.html.*

And he knew that he had a unique capacity, as the most powerful white politician from the South, to not merely challenge the convention that had crushed the dreams of so many, but to ultimately dismantle for good the structures of legal segregation. He's the only guy who could do it—and he knew there would be a cost, famously saying the Democratic Party may "have lost the South for a generation."

That's what his presidency was for. That's where he meets his moment. And possessed with an iron will, possessed with those skills that he had honed so many years in Congress, pushed and supported by a movement of those willing to sacrifice everything for their own liberation, President Johnson fought for and argued and horse traded and bullied and persuaded until ultimately he signed the Civil Rights Act [of 1964] into law.

And he didn't stop there—even though his advisors again told him to wait, again told him let the dust settle, let the country absorb this momentous decision. He shook them off. "The meat in the coconut," as President Johnson would put it, was the Voting Rights Act [of 1965], so he fought for and passed that as well. Immigration reform came shortly after. And then, a Fair Housing Act [Title VII of the Civil Rights Act of 1968]. And then, a health care law [the Social Security Amendments of 1965] that opponents described as "socialized medicine" that would curtail America's freedom, but ultimately freed millions of seniors from the fear that illness could rob them of dignity and security in their golden years, which we now know today as Medicare.

> I reject . . . cynicism because I have lived out the promise of [Lyndon B. Johnson's] efforts.

What President Johnson understood was that equality required more than the absence of oppression. It required the presence of economic opportunity. He wouldn't be as eloquent as Dr. King would be in describing that linkage, as Dr. King moved into mobilizing sanitation workers and a poor people's movement, but he understood that connection because he had lived it. A decent job, decent wages, health care—those, too, were civil rights worth fighting for. An economy where hard work is rewarded and success is shared, that was his goal. And he knew, as someone who had seen the New Deal transform the landscape of his Texas childhood, who had seen the difference electricity had made because of the Tennessee Valley Authority, the transformation concretely day in and day out in the life of his own family, he understood that government had a role to play in broadening prosperity to all those who would strive for it.

"We want to open the gates to opportunity," President Johnson said, "But we are also going to give all our people, black and white, the help they need to walk through those gates."

Debate About Equality and Opportunity Continues

Now, if some of this sounds familiar, it's because today we remain locked in this same great debate about equality and opportunity, and the role of government in ensuring each. As was true 50 years ago, there are those who dismiss the Great Society as a failed experiment and an encroachment on liberty; who argue that government has become the true source of all that ails us, and that poverty is due to the moral failings of those who suffer from it. There are also those who argue . . . that nothing has changed; that racism is so embedded in our DNA that there is no use trying politics—the game is rigged.

But such theories ignore history. Yes, it's true that, despite laws like the Civil Rights Act, and the Voting Rights Act and Medicare, our society is still racked with division and poverty. Yes, race still colors our political debates, and there have been government programs that have fallen short. In a time when cynicism is too often passed off as wisdom, it's perhaps easy to conclude that there are limits to change; that we are trapped by our own history; and politics is a fool's errand, and we'd be better off if we roll back big chunks of LBJ's legacy, or at least if we don't put too much of our hope, invest too much of our hope in our government.

I reject such thinking. Not just because Medicare and Medicaid have lifted millions from suffering; not just because the poverty rate in this nation would be far worse without food stamps and Head Start and all the Great Society programs that survive to this day. I reject such cynicism because I have lived out the promise of LBJ's efforts. Because Michelle [Obama, the First Lady] has lived out the legacy of those efforts. Because my daughters have lived out the legacy of those efforts. Because I and millions of my generation were in a position to take the baton that he handed to us.

Because of the Civil Rights movement, because of the laws President Johnson signed, new doors of opportunity and education swung open for everybody—not all at once, but they swung open. Not just blacks and whites, but also women and Latinos; and Asians and Native Americans; and gay Americans and Americans with a disability. They swung open for you, and they swung open for me. And that's why I'm standing here today—because of those efforts, because of that legacy.

And that means we've got a debt to pay. That means we can't afford to be cynical. Half a century later, the laws LBJ passed are now as fundamental to our conception of ourselves and our democracy as the Constitution and the Bill of Rights. They are foundational; an essential piece of the American character.

Progress Requires Hard Work

But we are here today because we know we cannot be complacent. For history travels not only forwards; history can travel backwards, history can travel sideways. And securing the gains this country has made requires the vigilance of its citizens. Our rights, our freedoms— they are not given. They must be won. They must be nurtured through struggle and discipline, and persistence and faith.

And one concern I have sometimes during these moments, the celebration of the signing of the Civil Rights Act, the March on Washington—from a distance, sometimes these commemorations seem inevitable, they seem easy. All the pain and difficulty and struggle and doubt—all that is rubbed away. And we look at ourselves and we say, oh, things are just too different now; we couldn't possibly do what was done then—these giants, what they accomplished. And yet, they were men and women, too. It wasn't easy then. It wasn't certain then.

Still, the story of America is a story of progress. However slow, however incomplete, however harshly challenged at each point on our journey, however flawed our leaders, however many times we have to take a quarter of a loaf or half a loaf—the story of America is a story of progress. And that's true because of men like President Lyndon Baines Johnson.

CHAPTER 3

Personal Narratives

A College Student and VISTA Volunteer Helps Communities in Arkansas

Linda Kelly Alkana

In the following viewpoint, a history teacher recalls the time in the mid-1960s that she spent in the VISTA (Volunteers in Service to America) program. She was genuine in her desire to improve lives and the world around her, she says, when she was assigned to an area of the South where out-of-towners with the government were not welcome. She was shocked to experience Jim Crow segregation in a little town in Arkansas. Her VISTA group eventually moved to a different Arkansas town, where they fit in better and worked with children at a Head Start program. She explains that they helped the community understand that the War on Poverty was undertaken on their behalf. She knew that she had made a real difference when the community thanked her at the end of her assignment. As a VISTA

Photo on previous page: President Lyndon Johnson (right) visits Tom Fletcher, an unemployed sawmill worker, and his family in Inez, Kentucky, in April 1964, a few weeks before delivering his Great Society speech. (© Everett Collection/Newscom.)

SOURCE. Linda Kelly Alkana, "Lunch in the Kitchen," *VISTA: In Service to America*. Washington, DC: Corporation for National and Community Service, May 2006.

volunteer, she learned much about herself and about different kinds of people and continues to apply those lessons in her life. Linda Kelly Alkana is a cultural historian who teaches history at California State University, Long Beach.

I'd been a VISTA volunteer back in Arkansas three years earlier. Now, in 1968, with a Civil Rights leader [Martin Luther King Jr.] murdered and many American cities in flames [due to race-related riots in cities such as Baltimore, Chicago, Detroit, Newark, and Washington, DC, in 1967 and 1968], my memories returned to Arkansas and to things I found as shocking as the assassination.

> I also joined VISTA because . . . I wanted to help make the world a little better.

I was 18 years old when I joined VISTA and had just finished my first year at UCLA (University of California, Los Angeles), majoring in International Relations. I joined because, as a recent immigrant from Canada, I could not join the Peace Corps. I also joined VISTA because, as corny as it sounds, I wanted to help make the world a little better.

My family felt a mixture of pride and anxiety with me leaving college and home. They expressed more concern when they learned I was assigned to Arkansas, which at the time was infamous for its prejudices and its governor's celebrated stand against the integration of a Little Rock high school.

Culture Shock in the Jim Crow South

I was assigned to Paris, Ark., with Mary Ann Smerdel. We were two white 18-year-olds, she from Indiana and I from California. It was the time of the Civil Rights Movement, and in Arkansas "out-of-staters" meant "agitators." We were two non-southerners in a world where teenage girls either lived at home or were married, and here we were, two kids representing the not-too-popular government. We were placed in this town without transportation or a job and in humidity we'd never experienced. Fortunately for us, fellow VISTA volunteer Jossie Hughes, a retired writer, was assigned to a town a few miles away and we could see her periodically.

Paris, Ark., was like a movie set. It was a small town (population: 3,000) built around a town square. It was in that town square that I had my first exposure to the layers of prejudice in the South. Segregation was everywhere. "Whites Only" signs hung on park benches and water fountains, and the seemingly more innocuous "We reserve the right to refuse service to anyone" messages were posted on restaurant windows. What surprised me more, however, was seeing black people get off the sidewalk to let a white person go by. I was outraged then, and I still am, to think that these wide, wooden sidewalks that framed the town square were a means of keeping some people "in their place."

Another event occurred a few weeks later that was equally as shocking. Mary Ann and I attended an introductory luncheon with VISTA bigwigs and some local Arkansas officials. One member of the Arkansas contingent was African American. He did not join us for lunch, but rather ate in the kitchen. In Canada and California I had read about segregation in schools, but never imagined it extended that far. I'll never forget my shock.

A Dedication to Social Change

It was the memories of these events that gave me perspective during the turmoil in the days after King's assassination. It is probably this perspective that affected my career choice. I decided to pursue a graduate-level degree in history. Taking a cue from the Civil Rights Movement, I studied social change and how people come together to fight for their rights. Even during our training, we VISTA volunteers had a sense that history was being made.

VISTA volunteers repair a screen door of a rehabilitation center in 1979. (© **Bill Peters/ The Denver Post via Getty Images.**)

Later, working on my doctorate degree, I studied those who were making it.

While in Paris in 1965, Mary Ann and I organized a clothing drive, accompanied a welfare worker on her rounds, and finally made friends with some of the young people of the area. We had little to do in Paris, and many of its citizens were wary of us, a situation further aggravated when a black VISTA volunteer from out of state visited us. So we moved to Scranton, Ark. (population: 229) and worked as VISTA volunteers in Head Start and the grade school. We fit in better in Scranton, which was a small German Catholic community (Mary Ann and I were both Catholic).

In Scranton, our involvement with Head Start was fun. We loved the kids. We worked with the teachers and coordinated transportation to the school. Because both the government and the town wanted to get this program implemented, all children in this small, white community were part of the program. Its immediate success allowed us to "work our way out of the job." We then became involved with the grade school system. In Arkansas, this was an era before any special school programs. Students either sank or swam. Mary Ann and I worked with students who needed help—we tutored, we encouraged, and we made friends. We worked in concert with the Superintendent of Schools and the teachers. With Jossie's help, we also linked teenagers with possible employers.

> We helped the community understand that the federal government was waging the War on Poverty on the community's behalf.

Making a Real Difference

The spirit behind the movements for social change that blossomed during that era's War on Poverty was immensely important. I think we made a positive impact in Scranton because we bridged the gap between the community, which was wary of the federal government, and the federal government itself. We helped the community understand that the federal government was waging the War on Poverty on the community's behalf.

Before we left, the citizens of Scranton called us to the school gym for a surprise "Thank You" award ceremony.

Mary Ann became such a part of the community that she stayed there and married a local boy.

I left Arkansas with a greater belief in my abilities and a better understanding of different kinds of people. I eventually returned to UCLA, got my doctorate in history and now teach a university course on the United States in the 1960s, in which I incorporate my experiences with the War on Poverty and my memories of the Civil Rights Movement.

Today my students often ask me what they can do when they graduate. I tell them about AmeriCorps and encourage them to discover its possibilities.

A Writer Reflects on the Effects of the War on Poverty on the Ozarks

Doris Weatherford

In the following viewpoint, a writer recalls the effects of the War on Poverty during her youth. She describes the poverty she experienced growing up in Arkansas and says she is grateful for President Lyndon B. Johnson's antipoverty efforts. She credits the War on Poverty with helping her family to move to a livable house as well as allowing kids to catch up in school and poor rural and urban Americans to get an adequate diet. She notes the irony that some of the states that gain the most from federal largess are also the ones more likely to oppose it in Congress. She also connects the War on Poverty to more recent federal projects in her area, pointing out that such investments—whether to help the poor or to build roads and dams—benefit the economy. Doris Weatherford is a writer specializing in the lives of American women. Her most recent books are *Women in American Politics: History and Milestones* and *American Women During World War II: An Encyclopedia*.

SOURCE. Doris Weatherford, "The War on Poverty," *Author's Guild*, January 13, 2014. Copyright © 2014 by Doris L. Weatherford. All rights reserved. Reproduced by permission.

I know from personal experience that great swaths of us won the War on Poverty. I grew up in the Ozark Mountains of Arkansas, where there were many hard-working but genuinely poor people—including (and even especially) white people whose families had lived in the South for generations. Yet we endured real poverty, sometimes not having the dime that school lunches cost. Especially in the late spring, before summer gardens were ready, some people did not have enough to eat. And this was past the mid-point of the twentieth century.

Many of those people, including some still alive today, have conveniently forgotten how impoverished we were in our youth, but we were in fact poor by any measurement. For example, just one of my half-dozen closest friends—the girls with whom I enjoyed slumber parties—had a bathroom that had been built as part of her house. All of the others used outhouses or unheated lean-tos added later, and we placed washtubs close to wood stoves for baths on Saturday nights. My dad arranged running water for us, but many of my friends' families pulled their water in buckets from a well. Again, this was in the early 1960s.

> Many . . . have conveniently forgotten how impoverished we were in our youth.

LBJ [President Lyndon B. Johnson] declared a war on poverty in 1964 because he was from Texas, and even though he married a wealthy woman, he never forgot his impoverished Southern roots. I shall be forever grateful to him and to his Democratic Congress, men who absolutely changed my life and those of countless others. Most of the members of Congress who voted for anti-poverty programs were not from the most impoverished states where oligarchy had reigned from the days of slavery, effectively enslaving both blacks and whites to generational poverty. These "blue" states still continue to support "red" states, which often bite the hand that feeds them, but [President] Bill Clinton and I and others remain grateful that these Yankees and their federal dollars gave us a shot at the American dream.

I'm especially thankful for the federal bureaucrat who happened to be a patient in the hospital where my mother worked. He made the effort to ask about her family and to tell her that we were eligible for a federal housing loan. He helped her fill out the forms; we hired a carpenter who lived nearby; and I went with her to shop for building materials. At last, we had a home that wasn't a fire hazard—for $32 a month. Long since paid off, that federal loan provided employment and sales opportunities in our community, and my sister lives in the house today.

> At last, we had a home that wasn't a fire hazard.

I also remember clearly when Head Start became available, helping kids catch up with their age group in other states that spent more on education. Yet even some educators wanted to refuse Head Start funds, arguing that this would lead to federal control of education. À la many Republicans today, they preached against "big government," doing their best to keep the ignorant ignorant, especially in economics.

One of the War on Poverty programs was food stamps, snappily re-dubbed SNAP these days, but few people realize that it was created as much for agribusiness as for its users. Leonor Sullivan, a Democrat from St. Louis, had both her urban constituents and Missouri farmers in mind when she repeatedly introduced a bill to require the Agriculture Department to use food that was rotting in warehouses—everything from corn to cheese that the USDA bought to keep prices high for agribusiness. She filed the bill for years after her 1952 election, and it was LBJ who signed it in 1964. With the federal subsidy of food stamps to use at their local grocery store, millions of Americans, both urban and rural, had an adequate diet for the first time in their lives. . . .

I was thrilled to use the new Crosstown/I-4 [highway connector in Tampa, Florida] link last week. I've wanted it since the 1980s, when I routinely dropped off my daughter for Girl Scouts in Brandon, rushed to the completed parts of the Crosstown Expressway, hurried through downtown streets to get to I-4, and then went on to the Westshore area for meetings of the School Board Citizen Advisory Committee at Jefferson High School. I so wished for a link from one high-speed road to the other—and now, much later, we finally have it. The road also will be a great boon to Ybor, as cargo trucks going to the port no longer will roar down its historic streets.

> We owe it to ourselves to invest in our future.

Please remember, too, that this construction was part of the federal stimulus package designed to pull us out of the [economic] crash of '08, when [George W. Bush] was president. That federal spending also continues to help Tampa's economy—and addresses genuine transportation needs—on I-275. And why shouldn't [we] help ourselves to this money? After all, a large portion of it comes from the visitors who clog our roads. We owe it to ourselves to invest in our future and theirs.

By the way, building I-40 [from North Carolina to California] was a big factor in ending poverty in the Ozarks. And the federal Corps of Engineers constructed a series of dams that made the Arkansas River navigable. Like the WPA [Works Progress Administration] money in the 1930s that built our treasured Bayshore, the world's longest sidewalk, these programs work.

An African American Man Discusses His Inability to Vote Prior to the Voting Rights Act

Hosea Guice

In the following viewpoint, Hosea Guice gives testimony before the US Commission on Civil Rights at a 1958 hearing in Montgomery, Alabama. He details to the commissioners how the local authorities have prevented him from registering to vote. He explains that he is a tax-paying, law-abiding farmer without any mental or physical disabilities. He says that he completed the voting registration application more than once but has been given the runaround by elections officials. One time they told him he missed a question, and other times he was just given wrong information about when or where he should meet with officials. He states that he is entitled to his right to vote, which has been denied to him only because he is African American. The need to address the issues described by Guice

---

SOURCE. Hosea Guice, "Testimony of Hosea Guice, Milstead, Macon County, Alabama," *Hearings, Montgomery, Alabama, 1958.* United States Commission on Civil Rights, December 8 and 9, 1958.

and many others like him across the South led to the enactment of the Voting Rights Act of 1965.

*V*ice *Chairman Robert G. Storey: Your name and age and place of residence, please.*

Mr. Hosea Guice: My name is Hosea Guice, fifty-five years old, born in Lee County, Alabama.

And how long have you lived in Alabama?

In Alabama all of my life.

Where are you living now?

In Macon County, Alabama.

At what place?

In Milstead Community, about thirteen miles out from Tuskegee.

And how long have you lived there?

Since 1942 at this particular place.

What is your business?

Farming is my business.

How long have you been a farmer?

All my life. Nothing else, only just little, minor jobs; but principally farming.

Is your wife living?

She is.

Have you any children?

Yes, sir.

How many?

I got three daughters, and, of course, another boy was raised there with me, related. I raised him.

He is a relative, then?

That's right.

Do you own your own farm?

Yes sir; I do.

What size is it?

A hundred and seventeen acres.

Do you mind saying whether it is paid for or not?

Not quite paid for.

Still a mortgage on it?

Yes; a little bit. A little bit.

Do you have your own farming equipment?

I do.

Paid your taxes?

> 'No, sir. I haven't found them [any mental or physical disabilities] yet.'

Sure.

Got any mental or physical disabilities, as far as you know?

No, sir. I haven't found them yet.

Have you ever been convicted of a crime?

No, sir; I haven't.

What is your education, if any?

Well, I finished the sixth grade. That's as far as I got—the sixth grade.

The sixth grade?

Yes, sir.

Did you go to work after that?

Well, I did. I went to work, the first farm work, see.

Can you read and write?

I can.

Do you take any newspapers or magazines and read them?

I sure do, every day.

Try to keep up with current events?

I do, every day.

Registering to Vote

Are you a registered voter?

No, sir; I am not.

Have you ever made application?

Yes, sir.

When?

The first application I made—the best I can recollect it was about 1954, I think it was, the first one.

Did you go to the board of registrars?

Yes, sir.

In your county?

Yes, sir; I did.

Did you go through a similar procedure as these other witnesses [testifying to the Commission on Civil Rights]?

I did, only except reading a portion of the Constitution. I wasn't asked to do that, see, but other than that I went through it.

And how long did you wait to see if you heard from that one before you did anything else?

Well, I never did go back to see about the first one. However, I come up to all the requirements that I was asked to come up to, but I never did hear anything from it. I didn't nurse [give special attention to] that first one that I made. I didn't go back to nurse it.

You didn't go back to nurse it?

Yes, sir, the first time.

All right. What did you do? Did you make another application?

I did.

When?

I made an application—the best I can recollect it was shortly—it was the last of January of 1957, I think it was.

Did you fill out new forms?

I did. I filled out another application.

Did they ask you to read or write anything?

Nothing but to fill that application out. They didn't actually—

The one like we introduced here?

That's right.

Given the Runaround by Officials

Did you ever hear anything from that application?

No, sir. Of course, I went back. After I thought I had given ample time, I—

About when did you go back?

About 2 weeks later.

Did you talk to any of the election officials?

Yes, sir. I talked to the gentleman—

Who?

One of the members of the board there.

Who?

In the person of Mr. Bentley.

All right. What did he tell you, if anything?

He told me—I asked him about my application; I didn't come out, and so forth. He told me—he says, "Guice, you missed one little question."

I asked him did I have a chance to correct it. He said I did. "When we meet again, you'll have a chance to correct it."

> 'He says, "Guice, you missed one little question" [on the voter application].'

That's the answer he give me.

Did you go back again?

No, sir; I didn't go back.

Did he tell you what the particular thing you missed was?

No, sir; he did not tell me that, and I—

And you haven't been back since?

I didn't go back because I would read or hear when they were going to get together, and when I'd get on my way up there or when I would go they wouldn't be together then, and, just through a misunderstanding, they just kept me confused, you see.

How many times did you go back?

One more time, after meeting him and talking to him. I went back for the particular purpose of investigating some more, but he—

Did you go back the time the board said it would be in session?

I did.

> 'I want to become a part of the government activity, and so forth.'

Or that you learned it would be in session?

That's right. That I learned they would be.

Were they in session when you went back?

No, sir. They weren't in session that day.

Exercising a Basic Right of Citizenship

Would you tell us why you want to vote?

Well, I feel like I'm entitled to it. I have come up to the other requirements to make myself a citizen, and I feel I would like to be a registered voter; they ought to give that to me. It's like I want to become a part of the government activity, and so forth.

You don't have any connection with Tuskegee Institute?

No, sir.

In any way?

No, sir.

Any other questions?

Commissioner Theodore M. Hesburgh: Just one. Mr. Guice, have you paid taxes all your life?

All my life? No, sir. Since 1942. . . . Every year since 1942 I have been paying taxes.

Commissioner J. Ernest Wilkins: What do you raise on your farm, Mr. Guice?

Principally cotton. . . . Cotton is the principal one. Corn and peas; all the things practically that goes with farming.

'I have . . . been a law-abiding citizen. . . . I was just a Negro. That's all.'

Commissioner Wilkins: Do you have any opinion, Mr. Guice, as to the reasons why you have never heard anything further about your application?

Well, I have never been arrested and always has been a law-abiding citizen; to the best of my opinion has no mental deficiency, and my mind couldn't fall on nothing but only, since I come up to these other requirements, that I was just a Negro. That's all.

The First Director of Head Start Recalls the Program's Origins

Julius Richmond, interviewed by Michael L. Gillette

In the following viewpoint, a former government official discusses the development of Head Start. After being appointed by President Lyndon B. Johnson to lead the Office of Economic Opportunity, Sargent Shriver created an advisory committee that came up with the concept of Head Start. The author discusses how the program addressed the issue of parental involvement as well as the multifaceted services Head Start provided to children and parents. Racial segregation was an important issue that affected the program's implementation, as was the role of middle-class families. Head Start, he says, is a product of the national commitment to the War on Poverty and reflects the character of the 1960s. Julius Richmond was a pediatrician, public health administrator, and Harvard Medical School professor. He served as the first national director of Head Start and was the surgeon general of the United States from 1977 to 1981.

SOURCE. Julius Richmond, interviewed by Michael L. Gillette, "Oral History Interview of Julius Richmond," Lyndon Baines Johnson Library, October 5, 1981.

Shortly after the Economic Opportunity Act was passed in the fall of 1964 and Mr. [R. Sargent] Shriver was designated by President [Lyndon] Johnson to take on the directorship of the Office of Economic Opportunity in addition to his Peace Corps directorship, he began to put together an advisory group to look at what could be done for young children that might have some impact on interrupting the cycle of poverty from generation to generation. My interpretation of the basis of his interest was the fact that he was more knowledgeable than most laymen about the impact of environment on the psychological and social development of children. . . .

When he became director of the Office of Economic Opportunity, building on his background he put together this interdisciplinary advisory committee to make suggestions as to what could be done to enhance the development of children growing up in poverty. This advisory committee was chaired by Dr. Robert Cooke, a pediatrician who was then the professor of pediatrics at Johns Hopkins. The committee suggested to him that it would be possible to try to develop a program that would provide for a comprehensive child development program. By comprehensive I mean that it wouldn't be just health and it wouldn't just be psychological, it wouldn't be exclusively educational or it wouldn't be social service, but rather it would put all of this together. And that's a remarkable document. There's a brief document, about two pages, I think, or maybe three or four, that that advisory committee submitted to Mr. Shriver, and it really laid out all of the things that subsequently came to be Head Start. . . .

Developmental Research as a Basis for Action

What we observed in very low income children that we were studying [at Syracuse University] from the prenatal period on was that they developed by standard tests reasonably well up through the first year. But at about the first year, when language becomes more important to development and as children begin to explore their environments and interact more with others, these children underwent a rather steep decline in development, again as measured by tests. Ultimately, of course, this gets reflected over the years in school performance because all of the measures that we're talking about are basic to performing in the usual school environment.

> We decided that it was worth trying to make a demonstration that one could in fact prevent this developmental decline [in low-income children].

Well, when we faced up to this naturalistic observation that these children were undergoing what we call developmental attrition, we then had to face up to the ethical question, since the parents didn't come to us for any intervention, should we try to intervene? We struggled over the ethical issues of whether we might be more intrusive than parents might desire, and we decided that it was worth trying to make a demonstration that one could in fact prevent this developmental decline, and we had demonstrated that. It was just prior to the time that the Economic Opportunity Act was passed. . . .

The Challenge of Parental Involvement

Bettye Caldwell [a colleague at Syracuse University] and I had had enough experience with parents to know that things went better if the parents were involved. We also learned that parent involvement with low income families was not necessarily what it would be with middle class families if you were going to have some impact, although I think we've learned subsequently even for middle income families that they do better if they're involved. The point of difference that I'm getting at is that with middle class families there had been a history of parent education. That is parents had some motivation, they wanted to learn about child development, they would be willing to sit in a classroom and have somebody talk to them about child development and the needs of children. We found that getting them involved in the actual program, letting them see what was happening, or letting them see how teachers worked with children was much more important.

We didn't have a clear idea of what we really wanted to see develop when we said parent involvement, and we tried not to be rigid about what communities submitted because we thought over time we'll empirically find out what seems to work better as communities explore this. But we didn't use the word "parent education" advisedly. It was on the basis of my experience in Syracuse and the best term that I could think of was "involvement," so that's what we stayed with.

Michael L. Gillette: Did you ever consider requiring, say, a certain measure of parental participation in order to enter the kids in a program?

Well, again, we didn't want to rule children out who were living in the worst circumstances. Our advisory committee was very alert to this. During that first summer and toward the end of the first summer, they kept saying, "Well, are we really getting the children who always fall between the cracks in those families that never get into programs?" We paid a lot of attention that first summer on how to contact such parents. For example, rather than relying exclusively on printed materials and the print media, we tried to do a lot over radio where we had some reason to believe that these families were more in tune with radio than they were with the print media. So we did everything we knew how to do, but we still had not satisfied ourselves at the end of the first summer that we were really getting the most needy of the children. . . .

In Head Start as it evolved when you came on, was part of the thinking to provide some sort of day care or did you consider what the parent might be able to do in terms of employment or generate income or something while the child was [at school]?

Oh, yes. Well, it had mixed goals and mixed objectives, and when I say comprehensive, if one pulls out the original pamphlet describing the program, though, and really what was sent out so that communities could respond, you get some of all of these objectives. Those that were child-centered, those that were oriented toward the parent, and particularly in relationship to social services, we proposed not to try to replicate what was available to families in the community. But we did specify that the Head Start program try to guide parents to the resources in the community: employment resources, welfare resources, social agencies that might be helpful beyond Head Start, the medical facilities in the community beyond Head Start. So all of these issues were initially part of the program, but I wouldn't say that we specifically designed Head Start so that mothers could be free to work. We felt it was inherently good.

> We did specify that the Head Start program try to guide parents to the resources in the community.

You must have talked to Lyndon Johnson about the Head Start program over the period that you were associated with it. I just wonder if he ever talked about the program from his perspective, what he thought of it.

I didn't have a great deal of conversation with him personally, more with Mrs. Johnson, but there were a couple of encounters that I had with him. At the time we made the first set of grants and I described our going over to the White House and his announcing them in the Rose Garden, Mr. Shriver and I went into the Oval Office together and he kind of shook his head and said, "You know, this whole thing is where I came in." I did a double take, and he said, "Well, you know, I'm a schoolteacher, I was teaching Mexican-American children. This program is designed to do what we were trying to do way back then and it just adds to what might be currently available." He, of course, was very intrigued, and interested and very committed. . . .

Head Start's Intersection with Civil Rights

How about participation in civil rights activities?

Well, there was a lot of that kind of activity. For example, we were cautioned—I was—by some of our security staff people, people from our Inspector General's Office about the problems of our riding in integrated cars, and I mentioned the rednecks. We were riding in integrated cars, but with the recognition that it was a very hazardous thing to do there at that time.

> "We were riding in integrated cars, but with the recognition that it was a very hazardous thing to do there at that time.

The contrasts, of course, are so great. Nine years later [in 1974] I was invited back to Mississippi to a governor's conference on education and youth and I decided, well, it'd be interesting to see how much change had taken place. Of course I went back and at the hotel in Jackson, Mississippi, there was the Governor with blacks on the platform and a lot of interaction. The whole meeting was integrated, the hotel was integrated and you had integrated professional staffs working in programs and all. So in nine years it was just a transformation.

So I mention that by way of indicating that the atmosphere was tense. The staff particularly that had come in from outside of the state was involved in civil rights activities. They viewed the integrated effort as an important step in civil rights. . . .

Was the fact that the program was largely a black program, that it was in fact segregated, did that create problems for you?

Well, it did in that we had intended for it to be an integrated program and we couldn't get it integrated. I think there was a sincere effort to get the poor white community to participate, but the climate of the times was such that, you know, there was no way poor white people were going to participate in a program that was predominantly black down there. So we never could quite turn that around until school integration really started to take hold in the South. . . .

> [We] wanted children from [middle income] backgrounds to interact with low income children.

The Challenge of Middle Class Participation

How about the participation of non-poor in the Head Start program? It evidently did appeal to a lot of people who didn't fit into the poverty bracket.

Well, the whole preschool educational movement, you see, it always had great appeal to middle class people and there just never was enough of it to satisfy their demand. So when this came along, we began—as a matter of fact, some of the most intense meetings I think I'd ever had were from middle class groups who said, "Why should the poor be the only ones to benefit from programs like this?" And that was a hard question to deal with. It was just more on the basis of need because we knew that middle class children would in the overall develop reasonably well, even if they did not go to [Head Start]. As a matter of fact that was an interesting thing. Bettye Caldwell and I had reviewed the data on early childhood education for middle class groups, and it was very difficult to see that it had really enhanced the development of the children. Their parents wanted it, and we didn't come out and say, "Well, you don't need preschool education for more affluent groups." But they do reasonably well even without such, although one could talk about social development and whether it doesn't add something.

So we did, however, feel that it would be desirable to have some mix and because we didn't want to be criticized for making it a program for the more affluent we limited that [to] 10 percent. Then there was some criticism of that. We did that with the notion that you wanted children from those backgrounds to interact with low income children and that that might be beneficial to both in social terms, but also in learning terms beneficial to the lower income children. But the data for really establishing that firmly had not been very good. We did that on the basis of impressions and judgments. . . .

The Challenge of Racial Integration

Let me ask you about Head Start as a tool for racial integration. You've touched on this in some cases, but do you think it was in general effective as such?

Yes, I think the fact that we came in in contrast to the public schools which historically had patterns set, we could learn from what had developed by way of segregation and try to minimize that. So we started out with a very conscious determination from day one to try to develop integrated programs. As I indicated, in some places we weren't initially successful, but we highlighted the issue and we kept working toward this and communities kept learning that we were serious about this. And we had our Office of Civil Rights with some people who were very ingenious. I began to learn the technology of civil rights enforcement, because they would tell me, "This application indicates they're going to run a segregated program," and I'd say, "Well, how do you know that?" They had built into our application form a map of how the bus routes would go, and they could tell from looking at a community, you see, whether that was going to be a segregated program or not. And that's how we didn't squander our meager human resources because we didn't have very many people who could go around and look at communities, but they could pretty much smell them out. I'm not sure, certainly it couldn't have been a hundred percent successful.

> There was a lot of national commitment to [Head Start] all the way from the top down to the grass-roots.

Were you successful in making segregated Head Start centers desegregated centers?

Well, we kept working at that. We wanted them to be integrated from day one, but you couldn't always accomplish that. But where they weren't, yes, we kept working at that. And over time I think there was reasonable success. . . .

A Reflection of 1960s Commitment to Progress

There was a lot of national commitment to it all the way from the top down to the grass-roots to the program that helped make it successful, from the President's commitment, Mr. Shriver's commitment, to the outpouring of volunteers. And in part, when I say the quality of the teaching was good, what you got essentially were teachers who were deeply committed, and of course that's a good part of teaching is the commitment that people bring to the task as well as the skills. And then the ingenuity of people to improvise. Again, if you just take physical facilities, I mentioned you couldn't use public schools in the South to begin with, so you had to find facilities of all kinds. And you had programs operating in just all kinds of improvised facilities, not always at a standard we would have liked, but workable nonetheless. . . .

One other point that I would make is that it's a lot easier to start programs from scratch then it is to turn old ones around to do new things. Having recently been in HHS [US Department of Health and Human Services] for four years, the contrasts are striking, but of course part of it is the contrasts in the periods: the sixties being a period of expansiveness, the seventies one of constraint.

The First African American Cabinet Member Reminisces About the Origins of HUD

Joseph Foote

In the following viewpoint, the author writes about the recollections of the first director of the Department of Housing and Urban Development (HUD). The author explains that HUD had eclectic origins and embodied two missions: to implement national housing policy and guide the development of US cities. As the first director, Robert Clifton Weaver had to establish the department, improve existing programs, get urban legislation enacted, and deal with urban riots that were partly caused by a dearth of decent housing. Weaver was the first African American

SOURCE. Joseph Foote, "As They Saw It: HUD's Secretaries Reminisce About Carrying Out the Mission," *Cityscape: A Journal of Policy Development and Research*, vol. 1, US Department of Housing and Urban Development, September 1995, pp. 71–73.

to hold a cabinet-level position, serving as secretary of HUD from its inception until 1969. Joseph Foote is the owner of an editorial and production services company in Washington, DC.

One who was present at the beginning recalls it as a time when "urban policy was bubbling up." The year was 1965, the ideas of the [John F.] Kennedy administration were riding the wave of President Lyndon B. Johnson's Great Society, and the future U.S. Department of Housing and Urban Development (HUD) was taking shape. . . .

The story of HUD over its 30 years can be told in many ways, but all of them begin with the Department's eclectic origins. Founded in the swirling events of the mid-1960s, only a year after riots in Watts racked Los Angeles and the Nation, the Department has carried out the dual mission of implementing national housing policy and guiding development of the Nation's cities and communities. The HUD Secretaries each interpreted that mission in his or her own way, worked with the President and Congress, and tried to advance the causes of decent housing and a rising quality of life for all Americans.

The Secretaries assumed responsibility for carrying out a mission crafted by Congress from those two broad pathways: first, to ensure decent housing, paying particular attention to those less fortunate in finding shelter; second, to encourage the healthy development of cities and communities nationwide, paying particular attention to economic development and quality of life. . . .

Robert Clifton Weaver

The first HUD Secretary and first African-American member of a Presidential Cabinet, Robert Clifton Weaver shepherded the establishment, organization, and initial staffing of the U.S. Department of Housing and Urban Development. HUD represented the country's

> 'We put a lot of things into operation that made it easier for [our successors] later on.'

first commitment to improving the quality of life in the Nation's cities.

In those early days, Secretary Weaver and his Under Secretary, Robert C. Wood, were "the builders, and there was a lot to be done," Secretary Weaver says today. They managed to get the Department established, began to administer programs that had been enacted just prior to its founding, improved existing programs, got solid urban legislation on the books, and dealt with urban riots. "We put a lot of things into operation that made it easier for [our successors] later on," Secretary Weaver says.

White House task forces were responsible for germinating important programs to be administered by the new Department, including the rent supplement program, enacted 1 month prior to the creation of HUD, and the Model Cities program of 1966. Both were controversial and had passed Congress by only narrow margins. Both relied on coordination among Federal, State, and local officials—a new concept in urban affairs—as well as decisionmaking by local residents.

In many cities, slum clearance had replaced dilapidated buildings with commercial construction or luxury apartments to attract the more affluent back to the city. But if a local urban renewal agency failed to find a developer for an assembled and cleared site it fell into disuse, sometimes for years. Many cities were experiencing both a net loss in low rent dwellings and a failure to attract upper income citizens. Secretary Weaver's response was to tighten regulations so that more low-income housing would be constructed on urban renewal sites. By 1968 the majority of new construction under urban renewal was undertaken for this purpose.

During 1967, together with officials at the White House, Secretary Weaver and Under Secretary Wood busily prepared new programs to provide decent housing

Robert Weaver was the first African American presidential cabinet member and the first director of the US Department of Housing and Urban Development (HUD). (© Francis Miller/The LIFE Picture Collection/Getty Images.)

for the urban poor. The growing desperation among the inner-city poor, as evidenced by riots in the Watts area of Los Angeles in 1965 and in Newark and Detroit during the summer of 1967 and by the erosion of support for President Johnson because of his stance on the Vietnam War, "shaped the timetable for these efforts," remarked Secretary Weaver. He and Under Secretary Wood over-saw the drafting of new housing bills and maneuvered them through Congress.

The riots of 1967 were followed by one of the stormiest years in American political history: the violent death of Dr. Martin Luther King, Jr., and the angry response within American ghettos, President Johnson's decision not to run for reelection, the assassination of Senator Robert F. Kennedy, the tumultuous Democratic National Convention in Chicago, Richard Nixon's hairbreadth victory over the rallying Hubert Humphrey, and deepening national resentment over the Vietnam War and the inflation it had spawned.

As the department most directly concerned with fair housing and housing for the poor, HUD became the focus of national attention following the April 1968 riots in Washington, D.C., Baltimore, Chicago, and elsewhere. In the aftermath of Dr. King's assassination, Secretary Weaver redoubled efforts to increase the production of subsidized housing units for lower income families. He and Under Secretary Wood testified forcefully on behalf of open housing legislation.

With the enactment of the Housing and Urban Development Act of 1968, the Nation acquired the most momentous Federal urban legislation in history. The law empowered HUD to establish Federal programs for crime insurance, flood insurance, New Communities, and the interstate sale of land. The law also partitioned Fannie Mae into a private corporation concerned with secondary mortgage operations and created another Federal agency, the Government National Mortgage Association (Ginnie Mae), to administer HUD's special assistance funds. Most significantly, the 1968 Act gave HUD the authority to administer new programs that would make possible homeownership by low-income families (Section 235) and would increase significantly the low-income multifamily housing stock (Section 236).

'The President counted on us to create a new Department . . . and we did.'

By the time he completed his tenure, HUD was an "ongoing concern," Secretary Weaver states. It had a home, a staff, and a nationwide network of offices. Most importantly, it had seen to the passage of landmark legislation to improve the lives of this country's low-income and minority citizens. As a testament to the commitment that Secretary Weaver engendered, none of the some 78 people—Presidential appointees, "Schedule Cs," and Civil Service personnel—who comprised his staff resigned during his tenure. "The President counted on us to create a new Department," Secretary Weaver says, "and we did."

CHRONOLOGY

1961–1963 During US president John F. Kennedy's administration, no significant civil rights legislation is enacted, but significant antipoverty legislation is passed, including increases in Social Security benefits and the minimum wage, the reintroduction of food stamps, and an expansion of school milk and lunch programs.

1963 August 28: The March on Washington for Jobs and Freedom, a massive demonstration for African American rights, is held in Washington, DC. Martin Luther King Jr. delivers his "I Have a Dream" speech.

November 22: President Kennedy is assassinated in Dallas; Vice President Lyndon B. Johnson is sworn in as president aboard Air Force One. At a joint session of Congress five days later, Johnson vows to pursue passage of a civil rights bill.

1964 January 8: In his first State of the Union address, Johnson outlines the antipoverty plan that becomes known as the War on Poverty.

May 22: Johnson gives a speech at the University of Michigan in which he defines the goals of a "Great Society."

July 2: The Civil Rights Act of 1964, legislation originally proposed by Kennedy the previous year, is signed into law; the act outlaws discrimination based on race, color, religion, sex, or national origin.

August 20: The Economic Opportunity Act of 1964, which creates agencies designed to fight the War on Poverty, is signed.

September 3: The Wilderness Act of 1964, which defines the mechanism for designating and protecting national wilderness areas, is signed into law.

November 3: Johnson is elected president with the largest popular vote in US history.

1965   March 7: Hundreds of African Americans marching from Selma to Montgomery, Alabama, for the right to vote, are assaulted by state and local police in an event known as Bloody Sunday. The president mobilizes the Alabama National Guard to protect the marchers, who finally reach the state capitol in Montgomery on March 25.

March 17: The Voting Rights Act is introduced in Congress.

April 11: The Elementary and Secondary Education Act of 1965, which provides federal funding and support for K–12 schools, is signed.

July 25: Johnson approves the escalation of US involvement in the ongoing war in Vietnam by increasing US forces from 75,000 to 125,000 troops.

July 30: Johnsons signs the amendment to the Social Security Act that creates Medicare and Medicaid.

August 6: The Voting Rights Act of 1965 is signed; the act regulates the administration of elections to enforce citizens' right to vote as dictated by the Fourteenth and Fifteenth Amendments to the Constitution.

August 11–17: Simmering resentments fueled by segregation, discrimination in housing, police mistreatment, and lack of opportunity boils over into deadly and costly riots in the Watts neighborhood of South Los Angeles.

September 9: The Housing and Urban Development Act is signed; the legislation increases federal funding for housing programs, provides subsidies for the elderly and disabled, and creates grants for poor homeowners.

September 29: The National Foundation on the Arts and the Humanities Act of 1965 is signed; it establishes a foundation to support national progress and scholarship in the arts and humanities.

October 3: Johnson signs the Immigration and Nationality Act of 1965, which abolishes national origin quotas, at the Statue of Liberty.

November 8: The Higher Education Act of 1965, which provides assistance for students in postsecondary and higher education, is signed into law.

1966   September 9: The National Traffic and Motor Vehicle Safety Act of 1966 is signed. The law empowers the federal government to set road and vehicle safety standards and creates the agency currently known as the National Highway Traffic Safety Administration.

October 15: The National Historic Preservation Act of 1966 is signed; the act creates the National Register of Historic Places, the list of National Historic Landmarks, and the State Historic Preservation Offices.

November 3: Johnson signs eight bills related to the Great Society in one day, including the Demonstration

Cities Bill, the Truth in Packaging Act, and the Clean Water Restoration Act.

1967   November 7: The Public Broadcasting Act of 1967 is signed; the act establishes the Corporation of Public Broadcasting, which gives birth to public television and radio.

December 15: The Wholesome Meat Act is signed to require federal meat inspection.

1968   March 31: Johnson announces he will not seek reelection.

April 4: King is assassinated in Memphis. The news sparks a wave of riots in a number of major US cities, including Washington, DC; Baltimore; Kansas City; and Chicago.

April 11: The Civil Rights Act of 1968, a continuation of the 1966 act, is enacted. The act includes the Fair Housing Act, which bans discrimination based on race, religion, or national origin in the sale, rental, and financing of housing. It also makes attacks based on the victim's race, color, religion, or national origin a federal crime.

June 6: Senator and Democratic presidential candidate Robert F. Kennedy is assassinated in Los Angeles.

August: The Democratic National Convention in Chicago is marred by party divisions, protests, antiwar demonstrations, violence, and police brutality broadcast live on television.

November: Vowing to restore law and order to the United States, Richard Nixon is elected president in a landslide victory.

1973   January: Johnson dies of a heart attack in the Texas Hill Country, the area where he was born, raised, and began his political career, and where he retired after the presidency.

FOR FURTHER READING

Books

John A. Andrew, *Lyndon Johnson and the Great Society*. Lanham, MD: Ivan R. Dee, 1998.

James Baldwin, "Nobody Knows My Name: A Letter from the South," *Nobody Knows My Name: More Notes of a Native Son*. New York: Vintage, 1993 (originally published by Dial Press in 1961).

Irving Bernstein, *Guns or Butter: The Presidency of Lyndon Johnson*. New York: Oxford University Press, 1996.

Nick Kotz, *Judgment Days: Lyndon Baines Johnson, Martin Luther King Jr., and the Laws That Changed America*. Boston: Houghton Mifflin, 2005.

Irwin Unger, *The Best of Intentions: The Triumphs and Failures of the Great Society Under Kennedy, Johnson and Nixon*. New York: Doubleday, 1996.

Edward Zigler, *Head Start: The Inside Story of America's Most Successful Educational Experiment*. New York: Basic, 1992.

Periodicals and Internet Sources

Joseph A. Califano Jr., "What Was Really Great About the Great Society: The Truth Behind the Conservative Myths," *Washington Monthly*, October 1999. www.washingtonmonthly.com /features/1999/9910.califano.html.

Carnegie Commission on Educational Television, "A Proposal to Extend and Strengthen Educational Television: A Summary of the Commission's Report," 1967. www.current.org/1967/01 /carnegie-i.

Peter Cove, "What I Learned in the Poverty War," *City Journal*, Autumn 2012. www.city-journal.org/2012/22_4_poverty.html.

Arne Duncan, "The Great Society, 50 Years Later," *Homeroom*, US Department of Education, May 2014. www.ed.gov /blog/2014/05/the-great-society-50-years-later.

Diana Furchtgott-Roth and Claire Rogers, "The Food Stamp Recovery: The Unprecedented Increase in the Supplemental Nutrition Assistance Program 2008–2012," Manhattan Institute of Policy Research, no. 23, September 2012.

Nikole Hannah-Jones, "Living Apart: How the Government Betrayed a Landmark Civil Rights Law," ProPublica, October 28, 2012. www.propublica.org/article/living-apart-how-the -government-betrayed-a-landmark-civil-rights-law.

Richard Jewett, "Mississippi Field Report," Civil Rights Movement Veterans, January 19, 1965. www.crmvet.org/docs/6501 _cofo_jewett.pdf.

Mike Konczal, "The Great Society's Next Frontier," *American Prospect*, November 19, 2012. http://prospect.org/article /great-societys-next-frontier.

Charles Murray, "The Two Wars Against Poverty: Economic Growth and the Great Society," *National Affairs*, no. 69, Fall 1982. www.nationalaffairs.com/public_interest/detail/the-two -wars-against-poverty-economic-growth-and-the-great-society.

"Johnson Signs 8 Bills Supporting Great Society," *New York Times*, November 4, 1966.

Dennis Roth, "The Johnson Administration and the Great Society," *Federal Rural Development Policy in the Twentieth Century*. Washington, DC: US Department of Agriculture Economic Research Service, 2002. www.nal.usda.gov/ric/ricpubs/rural_devel opment_policy.html.

Cecillia Wang, "Reflections of Another Affirmative Action Baby," *Blog of Rights*, American Civil Liberties Union, May 23, 2013. www.aclu.org/blog/racial-justice/reflections-another -affirmative-action-baby.

David Wise, "The Twilight of a President," *New York Times Magazine*, November 3, 1968.

Richard Wolf and Brad Heath, "Supreme Court Strikes Down Key Part of Voting Rights Act," *USA Today*, June 25, 2013. www.usatoday.com/story/news/politics/2013/06/25/supreme-court-shelby-voting-rights-alabama-congress-race/2116491.

Websites

The Great Society at 50 (www.washingtonpost.com/sf/national/2014/05/17/the-great-society-at-50). This site is a web portal to special coverage from the *Washington Post* on the history and legacy of the Great Society. The site includes in-depth news stories, archival and contemporary video, photos, and interactive data charts.

LBJ Presidential Library (www.lbjlibrary.org). The official website of the Lyndon Baines Johnson Library and Museum in Austin, Texas, includes a wealth of information about Great Society programs. The site provides access to online document and photo archives, summaries of important legislation and events during Johnson's presidency, as well as information about visiting or researching at the facility.

INDEX

Index

Generation X'ers, 84, 88

G.I. Bill (1944), 95–96

Gillette, Michael L., 154–163

Goodman, Andrew, 87

Government, big. *See* Big government

Great Depression (1929–1939), 13

Great Society programs
  educational benefits, 23–24, 94–104
  fiscal/moral irresponsibility, 61–71
  harmfulness for African Americans, 129
  Johnson, Lyndon, speech, 4, 17, 18–26
  legislation, 15*t*
  means-testing of programs, 62, 64–71
  New Deal comparison, 66–68
  Obama, Barack, commemoration, 124–133
  qualities, 21–23
  Reagan, Ronald, negative critique, 51–60
  successes/demographic changes, 72–82
  See also individual programs and legislation

Gross, Howard, 108

Guice, Hosea, 145–153

H

Hanks, Nancy, 107

Haskins, Ron, 69

Head Start Impact Study, 87

Head Start program
  benefits to low income families, 87–88, 132, 143
  Cheney, Dick, opposition, 85
  Commerce City, CO, *121*
  commitment to progress, 162–163
  description, 16
  developmental research, 155–156

  future directions, 123
  intersection with civil rights, 159–160
  means-testing basis, 68
  middle class participation challenges, 160–161
  Obama, Barack, comments, 132
  origin, 4, 14, 15*t*, 16, 117–123, 154–163
  parental involvement challenges, 156–159
  racial integration challenges, 161–162
  Reagan, Ronald, support, 85
  Republican party opposition, 85, 93
  research-based improvements, 122–123
  Richmond, Julius, interview, 154–163
  Scranton, AR, program, 139
  social values and mission, 120–122
  Weatherford, Doris, comments, 143

Heller, Walter, 44

Helms, Jesse, 109

Heritage Foundation, 65, 69–70, 111, 114

Higher Education Act (1965), 4, 15*t*

Higher education enrollment trends, *98*

Hispanic students, 100

House Ways and Means Committee, 36

Hughes, Jossie, 137

Humphrey, Hubert, 5

Hunger Prevention Act (1988), 33

I

Immersion Piss Christ (Serrano), *112*

Immigration and Nationality Act (1965), *10*, 15*t*

J

Jefferson, Thomas, 59

Jim Crow South, 127–128, 136–137

Job Corps, 4, 15*t*, 89

181